CASPAR DANTE'S
Book of
TORMENTATIONS

Caspar Dante's origins are as mysterious as the beginnings of time itself. He appears to have led a mystical and reclusive existence, choosing to emerge from his seclusion at certain moments in history to lead mankind a little further down the path of knowledge. Today we know him as Caspar Dante, but it is believed that he has revealed himself in many different guises and in many different places over the centuries. Only his loyal familiars – James Black and John Koski, Associate Editor of *YOU* Magazine – know the truth. And they are sworn to silence.

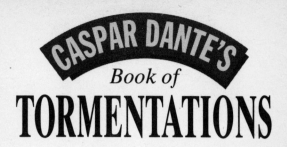

CASPAR DANTE'S
Book of
TORMENTATIONS

ASSISTED BY

JAMES BLACK
JOHN KOSKI

ILLUSTRATED BY

TREVOR DUNTON

CHAPMANS

Chapmans Publishers Ltd
141–143 Drury Lane
London WC2B 5TB

First published by Chapmans 1992

The right of James Black and John Koski to be identified
as the authors of this work has been asserted by them in
accordance with the Copyright, Designs and Patents Act, 1988

A CIP catalogue record of this book is available from the
British Library

ISBN 1 85592 736 5

Photoset by PerfectSense Ltd, Manchester
Printed and bound in Great Britain by
Clays Ltd St Ives Plc

CONTENTS

Welcome

To the first edition of Caspar Dante's *Book of Tormentations*, a tantalising compendium of essential facts and tormenting trivia culled from the pages of the *Mail On Sunday*'s YOU Magazine.

This book is dedicated to all the thousands of readers who have taken my page to their hearts and written in to me each Sunday discussing every topic it is possible to imagine.

Whether a puzzler or a wisdom-giver – thank you.

Long may our relationship continue.

Caspar

CHAPTER
ONE

WHY DO WE SAY THAT?

Why is New York referred to as the 'Big Apple'?

The 'apple' used to be jazz musicians' slang for a booking, or what they now call a 'gig'. New York, being at the time much the biggest and most important city in America, was the big apple, the date which every musician wanted. The term stuck because it sounded hip, and because it flattered New Yorkers who always like to be told how great their city is.

No one seems to know how the word apple first came to be used for a gig, though presumably like most slang half its purpose was to confuse outsiders who didn't understand it. I have never heard a modern New Yorker refer to the place as the Big Apple, any more than Londoners talk about the 'Smoke'.
Stephen Hogarth
Twickenham, Middx.

The name 'the big apple' probably became associated with New York through mis-translation by the Latino population of New York.

The word 'La Manzana' has two common meanings in Spanish, one being the term for block and the other being the word for apple. The Latin population possibly referred to New York as 'la ciudad de la Manzana Grande', which literally means the city with big blocks (buildings). This would be colloquially shortened to 'la manzana grande'. The English-speaking population has then translated this wrongly as 'the big apple'.

There are of course many other theories but I reckon this is the most sensible.
Alan Miller
Huntingdon, Cambs.

It gets its name because on a map it is shaped like an apple.
Tony Cowdrey
Wollaton, Nottingham.

The governor of the Dutch colony, Peter Stuyvesant, began planting apple orchards in 1647. In due course, the State of New York became famous for the quality of its apples. In the 1920's jazz musicians identified New York City with its rich variety of life, as the biggest and juiciest of all the State's produce and they coined the phrase.
Gordon Richards
Falmouth, Cornwall.

New York is called the big apple because it 'stems' from the 'core' of America.
Mrs Barbra Dean
Harrow, Middlesex.

New York is called the big apple because everyone would like a bite out of this exciting pulsating city, even though it could be rotten to the core.
Mrs M. Lester
Ilford, Essex.

Where does the expression 'take the mickey' come from?

To take the 'mickey' has its origins in the early 1900's when stereotyping of the Irish as being less intelligent was very common. As a popular Irish name at the time was Michael, this was shortened to Mick, or Mickey.
Sean O'Brian
Liverpool.

The term comes from the notorious 19th century figure, Mickey Finn of Boston, USA.

Mickey Finn was renowned for slipping mixtures into people's drinks in order to make them lose control, and do silly things.
Mr K. Borowy
Redbridge Park, Bolton.

It comes from Walt Disney's character Mickey Mouse and means anything that is fanciful or unbelievable.
Michael Mouse
Hollywood, California.

The expression has its origins in the early 1950's.

The common expression then, as now, for making someone look foolish was 'taking the p--s'. As in those more reticent days, such language was not acceptable in polite society, this was at first converted to 'extracting the urine'. This however was still considered too strong, and the original expression was then modified using a contraction of the word micturition, meaning 'to urinate' - hence 'taking the mickey'.
John Chipling
Staines, Middlesex.

FACT!

Michael Biggs, the son of the Great Train Robber Ronnie Biggs, is one of Brazil's top pop singers.

Who was Kelly and what was remarkable about his eye?

The term Kelly's eye originates from the Australian outlaw Ned Kelly, who wore an iron mask to protect both his face and his identity. He could see by the means of a single slit in the mask, which made it look like he had only one eye, not dissimilar to the cyclops of Greek legend.

Martin Bates
Denton, Manchester.

The original Kelly was a clown, a Mr Emmett Kelly who became world famous for his sad face and his hobo-like outfits.

Kelly used to draw straight dark lines from above his eye to the top of his cheekbone, this made his eyes look long and sad. From a distance they would resemble a number '1', hence the phrase, Kelly's eye. . . number one.

Jonathan Davies
Risca, Gwent.

Many of the bingo calls originated with the British Army before 1914, when the game was called 'Housie Housie'. Kelly's eye (for number one) was coined by artillerymen who did three weeks firing practice in the hills of Wicklow, Ireland, near a tavern which was kept by a one eyed Irishman named Kelly.

Mrs M. Clark
Bournemouth.

Edward Kelly was born in the town of Ballymahon, Co. Longford in the year 1857. Known far and wide as 'The Irish Cyclops' he toured the British Isles in a variety of freak shows and circuses. He had only one eye which was just right of centre above his nose. He was short sighted and had a special frame made to hold the solitary lens.

Mick Coplen
Mullingar, Co. Westmeath.

Why do Australians call us 'pommies'?

It's probably because the Australians can't spell 'British'!
John Lowis
Salisbury, Wiltshire.

There seem to be several different explanations as to why Australians use the term 'pom' or 'pommie' to describe the English. The oldest explanation is that 'pom' stands for 'prisoners of motherland'. However, D.H. Lawrence in his novel set in Australia, called *Kangaroo* provides a more pleasing answer. He claims that pommie is an abbreviation of pomegranate; which is rhyming slang for immigrant. Newly arrived British people on Australian soil also seem to turn red in the sun like a pomegranate. On a recent trip to Australia my mother was informed by Australians that pom stood for 'poor old migrant'.
John Burgess
Orpington, Kent.

In the days when we shipped 'undesirables' to that land, they would arrive with the tags 'Prisoner of His/Her Majesty'. This abbreviation of P.O.H.M. eventually became the Pomm of the Pommies that we are so affectionately called today.
Clive Hill
Leicester.

The name pommie for Brits in Australia is a derivative of the initials POHMIE.
This was supposedly printed on the exiled prisoners' suits and stands for Prisoners of Her Majesty in Exile.
Denise Blair
East Calder, West Lothian.

CASPARED?

What did the person who invented the drawing board go back to when he made a mistake?

6

Why is a pool of money called a kitty?

The name Kitty is a diminutive of the name Catherine, meaning 'pure'. Hence a pool of money or kitty is 'pure' (untouched) until it is won, doled out, or spent.
Mrs V. Thwaites
London SE17.

Calling a pool of money a kitty originates from the old Dutch word *kitte*, which was a tub. The money to be pooled would have been placed in a tub.
K.R. Malyon
Tunbridge Wells, Kent.

The word kitty comes from the Middle English word 'kist', from which we also get our modern word for 'chest'. A kist was a moneybox and the word was applied to the pool in a poker game. From being called a kist, it became the kit, and, finally, the kitty.
Miss D. Reynolds
Luton, Bedfordshire.

The word kitty probably comes from the corruption of the American expression CATER-CORNERED meaning at a diagonal but originally meant four cornered. This refers to the division of a card table into quarters in which each quarter was allotted for placing cards or money. Cater-cornered became corrupted to kitty-cornered and hence kitty for the part of the table in which card players placed an agreed amount of money to cover the costs of the game, such as drinks, food or a new pack of cards.
Nick Dickens
Manchester.

Kitty is a corruption of the French word 'quete', meaning collection. Thus, 'faire la quete' is to pass the hat around, or so to solicit voluntary contributions.
Brian Hardwick
Mirfield, West Yorkshire.

Why do we say it's raining 'cats and dogs'?

In Norse mythology the cat as the Devil's animal is supposed to have great influence on the weather. The dog is a signal of wind, like the wolf, both of which animals were attendants of the Viking storm god Odin. Thus the cat may be taken as the symbol of the downpouring of rain, and the dog of the strong gust of wind accompanying a rainstorm.
Jackie King
Royston, Herts.

It's an expression that's used to confirm that it's been 'paw-ing' with rain.
Euan Holt
Rothley, Leics.

CASPARED?

Why do tyres only ever puncture when it is raining?

In 16th century Britain the streets were so narrow and the drainage so poor that during very heavy rain the gutters would be awash with all kinds of debris including large numbers of stray cats and dogs which had died previously and been left to rot, or had drowned from the deluge itself.
Ken Auger
Yeovil, Somerset.

There is no record of it ever having rained cats and dogs, but it has rained frogs! This was due to a freak whirlwind scooping up fertilized spawn, which 'hatched' into tadpoles whilst whirling around. Two other 'animal' showers on record: In August 1892, in Padeborn, Germany, there was a snail storm and in July 1972, black worms about the size of bees fell from the sky by the thousands over Bucharest.
Miss I.K. Smith
Bury St Edmunds, Suffolk.

As I understand it, the saying originated from the urban conditions in Victorian slums and the emergence of a profusion of cats, dogs and rats, which took refuge upon the closely aligned rooftops.

When the weather took a turn for the worse, many of the animals were prone to be washed over into the street, hence the emergence of the expression.
Robert Sands
Seaford, East Sussex.

My favourite theory is that the phrase derives from the Greek 'catadupa' meaning 'waterfall'.
Janet Burholt
Dorchester, Dorset.

It is called this because afterwards we have to pussyfoot around to avoid stepping in poodles.
Mr R. Lloyd
Horfield, Bristol.

Why are the police called the Old Bill?

Old Bill was a walrus moustached, disillusioned old soldier in the First World War portrayed by artist and journalist Bruce Bairnsfather in his publications 'Old Bill' and 'The Better 'Ole'.

Cowering in a muddy hole in the midst of a massive bombardment, he says to his grousing old pal Bert 'If you know of a better 'ole, go to it'. The joke and Old Bill took the public's fancy and Old Bill became the embodiment of a familiar type of simple, cynical, long suffering, honest old grouser.
Rhoda Watson
Newtownabbey, N. Ireland.

The police are called Old Bill because in olden days when business was transacted, businessmen had to pay backhanders to various officials to 'smooth' the way. This was known as paying the 'bills' to do business. The one bill which was always to be paid was the police, thus it became known as the 'last bill'. After years and years, the last bill became known as the Old Bill.
Raj Tunvor
Middlesex.

The term Old Bill is rhyming slang which derived from a combination of the Law Courts, the Old Bailey, and the song 'Won't you come home Bill Bailey'.
John Gardner
Southsea.

FACT!

Most of the everyday policemen shown in the series *Hawaii Five-O* were actually real policemen who did the extra work to raise funds for the local police charity fund.

CASPARED?

Is a monkey wrench used to part monkeys?

Why are crusty old sailors invariably called 'sea dogs'?

The term 'sea dog' was first used in the golden heyday of England's supremacy on the high seas during the reign of Good Queen Bess - probably because our seamen were famed for pursuing and plundering treasure ships (usually the Spaniards) like predatory dogs. Francis Drake was the first to earn the title, which was soon thereafter bestowed on his other captains. It was extended to describe others who practised piracy (for that is what it was) on their own account, and finally the name was conferred on any tough old seamen - or 'shellbacks'. It became very popular among patriotic bards and ballad-singers, as a more romantic swashbuckling alternative to the tamer terms for sailors.
Bernard Campion
Plymouth, Devon.

Crusty old sailors get their name from being originally hunters (like dogs) and also from the fact they used to eat hard-tack biscuits which were similar to dog biscuits. It may also be worth saying that most old sailors had leathered faces and no teeth and looked very much like old dogs.
Cyril Goodall (ex-RN)
Wallingford, Oxon.

The saying relates to the sailors' gruff nature due to the weathering of their bodies and the lonely lives they had to endure.
Mrs D. Collins
Barry, South Wales.

Old sailors are called sea dogs because they used the ship's mast in the same way as dogs do a tree.
Ms Crisp
Colchester, Essex.

Why do we say 'as daft as a brush'?

The full version of the simile is 'As daft as a brush without bristles'. As a boy in the 1920's I heard the full version used many times by my great aunt - except that being an old Yorkshire woman she said 'baht brissles'. Those two additional words make the simile much more understandable, since a brush with no bristles is certainly a rather useless article. In recent years the expression has often become further corrupted to 'As daft as a brush and not half as useful' which makes the comparison rather more obscure than the shorter version!
Bill Hensman
Keighley, West Yorkshire.

The term originates from fox hunting and is used to describe someone who has been daft enough to leave a trail of mistakes that can only lead to them, like the fox who leads the hounds to himself by the scent of his tail (BRUSH). The person clever enough to escape the blame, like the fox who outwits the hounds, is described as being 'as sly as a fox'.
Andy Clark
Portsmouth.

The expression started life in the North as 'soft as a brush'. 'Daft' and 'soft' being interchangeable in meaning soon resulted in the expression becoming 'daft as a brush'.
Mrs I. R. Beal
Ipswich, Suffolk.

CASPARED?

What do occasional tables do for the rest of the time?

Have you ever met a graduate brush?
Michael Roberts
Norwich.

This one really puzzled me, so I decided to carry out some scientific research.

I sat down at the table having gathered around me my tooth brush, my hair brush, a rather balding yard broom, a carpet sweeper and a worn out 8" wallpaper brush.

I then asked them all the questions in the 'Baby Boomer' and 'Junior' edition of 'Trivial Pursuit'. I then tried them on the *You* magazine crossword.

The result was the same to every question. Absolute silence.

  Q.E.D. brushes aren't just daft, they are downright stupid.

Mr B. Dyke
Arnold, Nottinghamshire.

FACT!

In the world as a whole women nearly always live longer than men, but in Nepal the life expectancy of a man is one year more than a woman.

In the early 1900's unfortunate inmates of some mental asylums were expected to work in industry, often doing very menial tasks including sweeping up floors in the spinning mills. Most of them had problems conversing with the other workers and often behaved in a strange manner (in comparison to the staff at least) and because of this, someone commented that he/she was as daft as the brush they were using. This was abbreviated to as daft as a brush.

David J. Daly
Cookstown, Co. Tyrone.

The saying 'as daft as a brush' originated as 'as daft as Abrushi'. It refers to the antics of the Italian clown, Giuseppe Abrushi, the popularity of whom, I am told, spread through Europe to England where he toured the Music Halls in the early 1900's.

  My grandfather, who was the source of most of my information, often used the phrase in its earlier form.

Barrie Powell
Romford, Essex.

Why do we say 'Dressed up to the Nines'?

Because we British show more restraint than the French who dress 'up to the thirty-ones'! *(se mettre sur son trente et un)*.
Kenneth Mills
Hampton, Middlesex.

It's all to do with the price of admission to entertainment places of the past. The most expensive seats often cost 9d, and were referred to as the 'nines'.
To be dressed to the nines meant that one was fittingly attired for the best seats in the house.
Mrs V. Thwaites
London SE17.

The expression comes from the US Navy's system of numbering their uniforms. The order, dress of the day number nines, tells the crew to wear their finest ceremonial uniform.
Ian James
Haverfordwest, Pembs.

This expression is said by Walter Wilson Skeats, one of the greatest word sleuths of all time, to have come from a term going back many hundreds of years. Dressed to the *eyes* (meaning pleasing to the eye) would have been written in Old English as 'to then eyne'. It is easy to see how this has now become 'to the nines'.
  The saying gained further popularity circa 1850, when in military circles, a historical account of the Wiltshire Regiment noted that the 99ths' sartorial elegance set a standard that every other regiment was trying to emulate.
S. Mellors
Cramlington,
Northumberland.

Taking things to a scale of 1 to 10, dressed up to the nines is as near to perfection as you are ever likely to get.
Verity Nicholls
Dorking, Surrey.

Who was Larry and why was he so happy?

The expression 'Happy as Larry' originated in Australia. Larry was none other than the infamous Australian boxer, Larry Foley (1837-1917), who was dubbed the father of boxing down-under. Larry was undoubtedly a happy man as he was able to retire undefeated in bare-knuckle contests with a fortune of £1000 - all at the age of 42.
Simon Fox
Cambridge.

Larry was bound to be happy. Not only was he the only lamb ever to have his own television show, but he was also guaranteed to die of natural causes.
Diana Piercy
West Clandon, Surrey.

Larry is my wife's EX-husband and that is why he is so happy. . .
Mr P. Ballantyne
Havant, Hants.

Larry was in fact the Frenchman Count La Rie who owned a Chateau and vineyard in the Dordogne. He was always very happy. He also used to fall over a lot.
A. Mallett
Surrey.

CASPARED?

Why is a wrong number never engaged?

FACT!

During a routine patrol of the Queen's Gardens at Buckingham Palace guards were astonished to find a party of German tourists who had climbed the barbed wire fence and decided to camp out for the night thinking they were in a park.

What is the origin of the phrase 'I should Coco'?

The origins stem from Coco Chanel, the great fashion designer. Some of her clothes were so fanciful and outlandish as to be almost incredible, hence 'I should Coco' , meaning 'I would not be seen dead in that', 'not on your Nellie' etc. - basically something extremely unlikely.
Eileen Denham
Chatham, Kent.

Like so many of these type of phrases 'I should Coco' comes from good old rhyming slang. It began as 'coffee and cocoa', which meant 'I should say so'.
Sybil Edwards
Pelcomb, Dyfed.

CASPARED?

Who was the fool who lost the needle in the haystack in the first place?

I believe this to be rhyming slang:
'I should tell',
'I should Coco Chanel!'.
K.A. Beal
Ipswich, Suffolk.

I am sure the phrase is connected with the Russian born entertainer Coco the Clown and means 'I'm not going to look like a clown'.
Byron McGuinness
Oldham, Lancs.

This expression originated from the programme *Open all Hours* when Arkwright said to Granville, 'I should co-co-collar you, you little fibber Granville'.
M. Sutherland
Edinburgh.

It originates from the shortening of the phrase '*I should* be as surprised as if a *coco*nut were to fall on my head right now!'
John Weaver Smith
Ashford, Kent.

Why do people say 'touch wood'?

We say 'touch wood' because actually touching wood was an ancient superstition believed to avert bad luck. Certain trees such as oak, hazel, willow and hawthorn were sacred and so were believed to have strong protective powers. The actual type of wood has now become irrelevant and any wood is touched, and often, in jest, even one's own head.
John Wilson
Ely, Cambs.

It is supposedly symbolic of the cross of Jesus and by touching wood people are putting themselves under divine protection.
Ruth Pattison
Barmby Moor, York.

The expression to 'touch wood' comes from the practice of touching relics of the body or possessions of holy people in times of personal distress, to ask for blessing and relief. In the middle ages there was considerable trade in these holy relics, and a large number of fragments reputed to be from the cross of Jesus Christ were among them. This superstition has through time been changed in meaning and is now used to stop misfortune whilst hopefully bringing luck and prosperity.
Colleen Fleischmann
Cwmbran, Gwent.

CASPARED?

Why does time always go faster in a pub than it does at work?

FACT!

We spend fifteen times more money on dry cleaning in the UK than on the purchase of new bathrooms.

17

Why are condoms called french letters?

The name apparently originated during the First World War, with the Royal Flying Corps.

The use of the wind-sock first appeared on French airfields during this time and its tubular shape was immediately reminiscent of the contraceptive device. The wind-sock had an odd name something like *l'oeufil*, which the English troops had difficulty in pronouncing and characteristically referred to it in their 'Franglais' as Eff-ell. The sobriquet was subsequently applied to the similarly shaped condom, and ultimately shortened to F-L. Apparently new troops arriving in France, asked why they were called F-Ls, and the issuing officer, unable to offer the full explanation simply said it was short for 'French Letter', and the nickname stuck. Similarly German troops, who were also issued with condoms, had their own nickname for them. They called them Nahkampfsocken - meaning 'Close-combat socks'.
Frederick J. Stephens
Stony Stratford,
Milton Keynes.

For the same reason the French call them Capot Anglaise, which translated means English Overcoat!
Mr R.J. Bowen
Llantwit, Mid Glamorgan.

Can you think of a better name?
Jagdish Patel
Bolton, Lancs.

Simple, if they were called 'Welsh Letters', they would have leeks in them.
J.F. Moule
Darlington.

CASPARED?

Is impotency hereditary?

Who was Buggins and what did he get when it was his turn?

Buggins was the name given to a notorious Victorian alcoholic who frequented London public houses. Hence 'he who "bugs" inns'. What he got was a helping foot back onto the cold cobbled street.
Mr R. F. George
Pensby, Wirral.

Buggins' Turn is an appointment made because it is somebody's turn to receive it rather than because he is especially well qualified to. The name Buggins is used because it sounds suitably dull and humdrum.
Mr E. Lloyd
Wigan, Lancashire.

The name is a derivative of Bilbo Baggins, who got the satisfaction of getting 'There and Back Again' (which is indeed the subtitle of that event as encountered by the hobbit).
Sarah Coffey
Eastleigh, Hampshire.

Buggins is an apprenticeship boy in *Half a Sixpence*. When it was his turn he got a meerschaum pipe.
S. Wright
Bedworth, Warwickshire.

CASPARED?

Where does a tickle go when you scratch it?

FACT!

The FA Cup Final of 1933 between Everton and Manchester City was the first game in which players wore numbered shirts. The numbers 1 to 11 were worn by Everton and those from 12 to 22 were worn by Manchester City.

Why do we say 'bless you' when someone sneezes?

The answer lies with past outbreaks of bubonic plague where the symptoms were fever, the swelling of the lymph glands and in the first stages of infection, sneezing. As the plague was at the time incurable, it was natural for sneezes to be answered by wishes of God's protection - hence 'God Bless You'. That is of course if the people in the vicinity of a plague sufferer stayed around without fearing contamination.

This saying still echoes in children's playgrounds with the song to a game:

Ring a ring o'roses,
A pocketful o'posies,
Atishoo, atishoo,
We all fall down.

A ring of roses portrayed the physical marks of infection, the pocketful of posies were the herbs used to ward off infection, the sneezes were the symptoms and the all fall down, meant death.

Martin John Faulkner
Northwich, Cheshire.

If anybody sneezed on my new clothes, they would definitely need blessing if I got my hands on them.

Doreen Maxwell
Willesden Green, London.

The practice of saying 'Bless You' after somebody has sneezed is believed to originate from Pope Gregory the Great in the 6th century who recommended its use after an outbreak of plague in Rome and called for prayers as protection against infection.

Barbara Watson
Sandy, Beds.

It used to be thought that when someone sneezed their heart momentarily stopped beating. In order to ensure that it did not become a permanent stoppage all those within hearing, and spraying, range said, 'God Bless You'.

Andy Frost
Callington, Cornwall.

When a person sneezes, the effort and energy required makes the bodily functions almost stop and takes a person close to death. It is at this point that the Devil is thought to come out of the body at this time. The blessing given by someone who says 'bless you' restores the supremacy of God to what would be an otherwise catastrophic situation.

Robin Stevens
Chelmsford, Essex.

It has been traditional for many hundreds of years to say 'bless you' to anyone who sneezed. This is because it was originally believed that the force of a sneeze forced the soul from the body. Anybody who was nearby when they heard a sneeze would try to remedy this situation using these words, thus helping the soul find its way back.

Heather Ditch
New Malden, Surrey.

How did the saying 'put a sock in it' originate?

In about 1887 Emil Berliner produced the first gramophone to play disc records. The sound emerged through a large horn, and much later from a resonance box, both of which greatly amplified the sound. However, the one thing that was missing was any form of volume control. The most popular way of regulating the sound was to literally 'put a sock in it'. A woollen sock was placed inside the horn, or resonance box, to reduce the volume. If the recording was particularly loud, many socks would be required. Gramophones were still being stuffed as late as 1930.
Colin Cutler,
Billericay, Essex.

The saying 'put a sock in it' originates from washing machine manufacturers who, when testing their machines on April 1st, decided to play a joke on the consumer by adding a special mechanism to their machines.

Thus, every time they were used, a sock would go missing, leaving an odd one. The answer to this question, therefore, solves two mysteries instead of one!
Miss A. Whitehead
Rainham, Essex.

The origin of the saying 'put a sock in it' can be easily answered by anyone who has served in the Armed Forces. It is common practice for soldiers to house their mess tins, knife, fork and spoon in the two kidney pouches placed at the rear of their webbing.

Unfortunately these metal objects tend to create a most unwelcome noise, banging together every time you try to move.

In order to remedy this situation, a pair of socks (preferably clean) were wound round the offending items, thus stopping the noise.
Martin Pankiewicz
Colchester, Essex.

What is the origin of the phrase 'Going Dutch'?

'Going Dutch' refers to a 'Dutch treat', an entertainment at which everybody pays their own share, first recorded in 1875. Many similar phrases, often derisory, stem from the Anglo-Dutch wars of the 17th century, when there was intense trade rivalry and naval jealousy.
John Deamer
Broadstairs, Kent.

The Dutch in the phrase came from the Netherlands which when translated means Lowlands. 'Going Dutch' means lower bills for more people, rather than one high bill for one.
Melody Lewis
London.

The origin of 'going Dutch' comes from the USA. Dutch settlers held parties, lunches, suppers and treats among themselves, where each person contributed their own share or portion.
'Dutch' as an adverb means 'with each person paying for his own share'.
John Deering
London.

FACT!

Alfred Nobel, the founder of the Nobel Peace Prize was also the inventor of dynamite.

CASPARED?

If woolly jumpers shrink when wet, how come sheep don't?

FACT!

When the Volcano Krakatoa exploded in 1883 it caused a tidal wave that reached as far as Cape Horn, almost 8000 miles away.

Why are unwanted objects called 'white elephants'?

There is an elephant native mainly to Thailand which is whitish or pale in colour. Also, within the Buddhist religion the white elephant is a sacred animal. At the time when Thailand was called Siam, its kings would keep white elephants because of their sacred position. They were kept in absolute splendour. Indeed, King Phra-Narai's elephant was fed only from a golden vessel.

The kings of Siam, if they wanted to ruin a person, could do so by giving a gift of a white elephant to that person. Even though it was given in honour it would be the ruin of the person because he could not dishonourably give the gift away, but could also not afford the great expense of keeping such a sacred animal in splendour.
Mr N. M. Dickens
Manchester.

The truth of the matter is that in the 11th century India, when car boots were still at the drawing-board stage, the peasants often disposed of their unwanted household goods with a sale from the back of an elephant. The elephants tended to turn white with fear when hordes of marauding bargain-hunters appeared, and were thus the very first 'White Elephant Stalls'. The phrase 'white elephant' was subsequently applied to any unwanted item.
Mrs A. J. Trimble
Wilmslow, Cheshire.

We call unwanted objects white elephants because we usually find them hidden in large dusty trunks!
Mrs Lynn Cunningham
Hull.

Why do we 'paint the town red' on a night out?

The phrase originated in the Leicestershire town of Melton Mowbray and refers to a mad escapade which took place in the early hours of Thursday 6 April 1837. It was the time of the Croxton Park Races and many of the hunting fraternity (many with 'Royal' connections) were in residence in the hunting lodges in and around the town. One of these was the Marquis of Waterford.

Early in the morning, the Marquis and his friends who were undoubtedly out for a good time began to run amok. Hurling through the town, they attacked the local constable and then rampaged down the Beast Market (Snerard Street). One of their number carried a large tin of red paint and the others carried brushes. They smeared red paint over the front doors of several houses, wrenched off doorknockers and damaged flower pots, etc.

Paint was spread over the front of a draper's shop and over the brass door plate of Judd's Bank. In the Market Place, the sign of the Old White Swan Inn soon became red, most of the houses in this part of town ended up covered in red paint and the post office letter box was given a coat of paint. Windows were screwed down, others were smashed and numerous other similar outrages were committed. The local watchman, Barnes, ended up covered with red paint himself. Hence the expression 'paint the town red'.

Many of the revellers were later caught, sent to Derby assizes, and were eventually fined £100 each on charges of assault

David L. Bland
Bushey, Herts.

We say it because we have a **bloody** good time, it involves **scarlet** women and **cardinal** sins and ends up with us **marooned** somewhere, with **crimson** eyes, and a **blushing** face. To top it all we spend so much money we end up very much in the **red**!
Enid Collins
Hereford.

In the days of the Wild West, cowhands who had been on the trail for many months without female company headed straight for the first town's red light area. In a small town, a large number of rejoicing cowhands would monopolise the town with their 'red-light' behaviour.
Chris Bradley
Bracknell, Berkshire.

We paint the town red on a night out so that all the traffic stops, allowing us to stagger across the road safely.
P. J. Ford
Hatfield, Hertfordshire.

What actually happens is the alcohol, the cigarette smoke and the late hours combine to give us bloodshot eyes. Therefore everything looks red.
Linda Fisher
Gloucester.

CASPARED?

At football grounds, why are all seated areas called stands?

FACT!

The actor Oliver Reed worked in various occupations before becoming a star, including bouncer, boxer, and taxi driver.

CASPARED?

If margarine is better for us, why is it always made to look like butter?

Why do we call people toffee-nosed?

Because the snobbier people are always the ones who aspire to live on Quality Street!
Norman Mundgros Inniskillen.

This dates back to the late 19th century. When the working classes attended a travelling circus or fair, they were able to choose between plain or toffee covered apples sold by the vendors. The toffee apples were a little more expensive and the snobbier families would always buy one, making sure that a sticky residue remained around their mouths and nostrils as a kind of status symbol. The practice soon died out, mainly because most people were unimpressed by such displays and coined the phrase 'toffee-nosed' to describe those people who had ideas above their station.
James Rhy Davies Sketty, Swansea.

The term derives from 'toff', meaning a stylish or smart person. 'Toff' is a variation of toft which is an alternative word for 'tuft' as applied to nobles and gentlemen at the universities of Cambridge and Oxford.

The 'tuft' is the gold tassel on the cap worn by titled undergraduates. They had to tilt their heads back in order to prevent the tassel from dangling over their noses. Hence the term 'totty' or 'toffee-nosed'.
Jackie Brown Rubery, Birmingham.

People who eat toffee often get it stuck at the top of their palate and lift their chin and nose into the air in order to remove the toffee from the top of their mouth with their tongue.

As the same action is used by people who, thinking themselves better than others, lift up their noses we end up with 'toffee-nosed'.
Mrs A. Tonkinson Shifnal, Shropshire.

What is the origin of the phrase 'the full monty' and has it got anything to do with Field Marshal Montgomery?

It originated in the dockland area of Salford, Lancashire in the 1940's when money and clothing were hard to come by.

The tailors, Montague Burton, issued £5 vouchers to be spent in their shops. These were to be repaid at a couple of shillings a week. The customer could then buy the full 'monty' of suit, shirt, and other items.

Mr D. Scaife
Nether Poppleton, N. Yorks.

The MONTY here derives from MONTESSORI, rhyming slang MONTESSORI - STORY. So, the FULL MONTY means the FULL STORY. This has nothing therefore to do with Field Marshal Montgomery.

Janet Burholt
Dorchester, Dorset.

The answer can be found in the Kingsley Amis novel *Take a Girl Like You*, where a wondrous party spread is referred to as the full Monte Carlo, meaning the definitive form of luxury.

Richard Banfield
Hemel Hempstead, Herts.

Montgomerie was the leader of a band of French brigands, who always kept for himself any booty that was taken; thus the full monty came to mean having everything.

Mr E. Piper
Tilehurst, Reading.

FACT!

Without the aid of communication equipment it is impossible to hear sound in outer space.

Why are doctors known as quacks?

During the bubonic plague, doctors wore big leather coats and masks to keep the germs away from them when treating patients. The mask had a 'beak' stuffed with sweet smelling flowers so the doctor would not smell the vile stench of the disease. It was believed flowers (and herbs) would help ward off plague as at the time it was thought that the illness came from the smell of disease. The beak the doctor wore made him look like a bird or duck, and since ducks go quack it is only reasonable to assume this is how the doctors got the nickname.
Kirsty Hunt
Farnham, Surrey.

Because like a duck, he can stick his bill up his bottom.
George Lewis
Worcester.

Because the majority, whilst at school 'ducked' writing lessons.
Peter Hughes
Loughborough, Leics.

The word quack as applied to doctors has nothing to do with the sound made by a duck. It is in fact an abbreviation of the 16th century word, quacksalver, derived from the Dutch quack, meaning to hawk and saif, an ointment for sores and wounds.
In other words, a quacksalver was a person selling ointments, which were probably useless. These days the word has become a more general and jovial term for a doctor.
Dr E.J. Sandford
Llansanffraid, Powys.

This obviously comes from the time when patients paid their doctors for treatment before the NHS. There were varying degrees of quacks, from the small to the outrageous - this all depended of course on the size of their bills!
Lesley Boyd
Bracknell, Berks.

CHAPTER

TWO

THE HUMAN CONDITION

What is the difference between 'stable', 'comfortable', and 'satisfactory' in the bulletins given out by hospitals?

The terms used by hospitals are in the main self explanatory.

'Satisfactory' means that the doctors are satisfied with the progress - unlikely if the patient is gravely ill.

'Comfortable' indicates the patient is not experiencing a great deal of pain.

'Stable' means that although the condition may be serious, it is not deteriorating.

Of course, with the state of the NHS at the moment, being in a stable condition may well mean that the ward has not been mucked out recently, and that the meals are served in nosebags.
Mrs L. Whiteside SRN
Bournemouth, Dorset.

All registered nurses work under a strict code of conduct. One of the clauses of this code is that of confidentiality which prevents nurses revealing too much information about the patient without their prior consent. The words are as general as possible and used only to give a rough idea of the condition of the patient whilst being as reassuring as possible.
Claire Stringer RGN
Kennington, London.

In these trying times for the NHS, the terms mean as follows:

Stable - No change. Still lying on a trolley in the corridor waiting for a bed.

Comfortable - Finally lying in a bed.

Satisfactory - Well enough to be considered fit for a removal to another hospital.
Janet Burholt
Dorchester, Dorset.

Why do men have nipples?

Because human embryos start their existence as female, only developing male bits as the pregnancy progresses, if the right level of male hormone is present. Secondary sexual characteristics such as nipples therefore remain. (So much for Adam's rib, eh!)
Jane De Gruchy
Letchworth, Herts.

So that women don't come as a complete surprise.
Alan Lewis
Naphill, Bucks.

How else would they know where to take a chest measurement?
Mrs Janice Loveday
Buckinghamshire.

To hang their keys on when they are sunbathing.
S. A. Warren
Hinckley, Leicestershire.

Everybody knows men have nipples to stop their chests from fraying.
Bryan Richardson
Guildford, Surrey.

Nipples are like the tool kit that comes with a Rolls Royce. Although you'll never need to use them, they're there just in case.
Tim Bean
St. Peter Port, Guernsey.

The reason men have nipples is because nature, like the most efficient industries, uses mass-production techniques. It is simpler and quicker to 'put' nipples on all human beings rather than 'stopping the process' and determining whether the end result is male or female.
D. Fisher
Maidenhead, Berks.

Men have nipples so that they can do a convincing impersonation of Kylie Minogue.
Maurice Batust
Norfolk.

So that women can tell which side of their man is the front.
Mr T. A. Blackman
Ipswich, Suffolk.

Why do fingers go wrinkly in the bath?

The outer layer of the skin, the epidermis, is composed of layers of cells which are themselves mainly formed from a protein called keratin. One of the physical properties of keratin is to swell and expand in the presence of water.

When we wash our hands, especially in hot water, the keratin in our skin absorbs a little of the water, and expands, throwing the surface of the skin up into the characteristic folds and wrinkles.

The wrinkling tends to be confined to the fingers, the palms, and soles of the feet, as the skin in these areas has the thickest superficial layer of Keratin, in order to protect our hands and feet from excessive friction damage.

Martin King
Exeter, Devon.

Surely it's to enable us to get a better grip on the soap.
Mrs S. Howard
Bootle, Merseyside.

The scientific explanation is that it is due to a process called osmosis. Basically this means that water will 'diffuse' from the bath through your skin. The skin cells then expand with extra moisture and your skin takes on a 'bloated' appearance.
Rachel Ince
Scunthorpe, South Humberside.

When you are in the bath your skin acts as a semi-permeable membrane, expanding and wrinkling as it absorbs water. Conversely whilst in salt water i.e. swimming in the sea, the salt draws water through the skin causing it to shrink and therefore wrinkle.
Simon Morton (Age 14)
Sevenoaks, Kent.

Fingers go wrinkly in the bath so you know when it is time to get out!
Sasha Knowles
Richmond, Surrey.

What causes spots before your eyes?

Having breakfast with four teenage sons.
John Sutcliffe
Bingham, Nottinghamshire.

The spots show up mostly on light backgrounds and are caused by cellular debris floating in the 'aqueous humour' in the eyeball. If these cells, or strands of cells, position themselves near the retina they come into focus or cast shadows and show up. In extreme cases they can be distracting and worrying but they are of no clinical importance and if troubled by them, one has to live with them and try to ignore them.

I am 71 and have been troubled by them for about 30 years.
John Verney
Gwynedd, Wales.

A smack on the head with a hammer!
David Serf
London.

Muscae volantes is the medical term for the peculiar little floating images which everyone sees before their eyes from time to time. The Latin name means 'flying flies' and they are caused by opaque particles being trapped in the body of the eye. They are said to be tiny fragments of placenta and have therefore been there since birth. The 'flies' can appear as spots and straight and looped fibres, which cast their shadows, enormously enlarged upon the retina of the eye. The brain then projects these images into space and thus they appear to be floating in the air, especially when viewed in bright light.
Mrs E. Marshall
Lincoln.

CASPARED?

Is red cabbage green grocery?

Falling asleep into your bowl of Sultana-Bran.
Mrs K. Bridges
Beckenham, Kent.

The answer lies with having a husband, two sons and satellite T.V.!!!
  Sorry, I thought you said SPORTS before the eyes.
Mrs M. Raper
Sunderland.

The cellular debris float not in the aqueous humour which is a watery fluid lying in front of the lens of the eye, but in the vitreous humour which is a more viscous fluid lying behind the lens. 'Muscae volantes' are not tiny fragments of the placenta but may be part of the hyaloid artery which nourishes the eye during the foetal stage. How can a bit of placenta get inside the eye?
Antony Socrates
Royal Victoria Hospital
Bournemouth.

CASPARED?

Why is there only one monopolies commission?

FACT!

After being killed at the Battle of Trafalgar in 1805, the body of Horatio Nelson was shipped back to England preserved in a cask of brandy.

FACT!

The hardiest tree in the world must be the Ombu tree of Argentina. It can live for months without water, can survive massive insect attacks, violent storms and intense heat. The tree is so moist it will not burn and so spongy it is virtually impossible to cut down with an axe.

FACT!

When Barbara Castle became minister of transport in 1965 she didn't have a driving licence.

When we have a cold, why doesn't our nose run when we are asleep?

When we have a cold, our mucus is produced by goblet epithelial cells which line the inside of our nose, throat, and upper bronchus.

At times of infection these cells increase in number and size and produce large amounts of mucus.

At night our noses do not run for two reasons, the first being that as we lie down, gravity cannot exert its effect on the mucus and it is retained in the nose to congeal as we sleep. The second reason is that at night our metabolic rate falls and thus much smaller amounts of mucus are produced.

David Meech
Heaton, Bradford.

It's obvious. When the tooth fairy does her rounds she first disposes of teeth, then, when finished gets some overtime in with wads of cotton wool, plugging away.

W. J. Honeywood
Norwich.

Even germs have to rest, and they prefer, if possible, to let you have a good night's sleep as well. In this way, you will be able to appreciate all the more keenly the misery they cause in the morning.

Graham Russet
Redruth, Cornwall.

If your nose runs and your feet smell then you must be sleeping upside down.

Paula Greaves
Solihull, West Midlands.

Exactly what kind of a cold does the questioner suffer with? 'Daytime only colds' are news to me. If I have a cold, the accompanying runny nose runs, regardless of whether it is dark or light outside.

Maybe it's just another symptom that only we in Essex seem to suffer with!

Cherie Fullerton
Essex.

Why is it that when your hair is wet or greasy it goes darker?

Hair colour is determined by a pigment called melanin, the same pigment that determines skin colour. When dry, or non-greasy, most hairs are free to move independently of one another, leaving gaps and air spaces between each strand of hair. When white light falls on to the hair, the melanin absorbs some of the colours of the visible spectrum, reflecting back to our eyes the remaining parts, as well as mixing with it any white light which has passed through the gaps in the hair, and light which has been reflected from the scalp. When hair is wet or greasy, the strands stick together and leave very few air spaces between them. As a result, only light reflected from the hair is seen, with no mixture of white light passing through the air spaces in dry hair. The result is that the hair seems to have a much darker appearance, which is in fact a much more accurate reproduction of the true colour of the melanin of the hair.

Martin O'Regan
Solihull, West Midlands.

The darker colour of wet or greasy hair is an illusion caused by the absence of light-shafts through the hair. When the hair is dry the light penetrates between the separate hairs thereby giving the strands a light colour. When the individual hairs are compacted by water or grease little light can penetrate, thus producing a darkening effect on the hair. Not surprisingly, bald people are immune to this phenomenon.

Mr K.H. Stock,
Cleveleys, Blackpool.

Do people blind since birth dream in the same way as sighted people?

Dreams are, of course, a mish-mash of factual and fictional memories, hopes and fears for the future, warnings and promises from the sub-conscious. I don't think the dreams which blind people experience are much different from those of the sighted. Returning to the consciousness is, of course, different for a blind person. Living with your eyes pemanently shut differs from the option to open them.
John Wall
(Blind since birth)
London.

FACT!

In Britain, we spend over twice as much money on greetings cards than we spend on funerals.

Being sighted I don't know, but I once asked a German friend who was completely tri-lingual (in German, English, and French) which language she dreamt in. Her reply was that dreams involving success and riches were usually in German, those in which she was cold, tired, or depressed were in English, and those being rude were invariably in French.
Kerry Harvey-Piper
Thriplow, Herts.

One's dreams reflect one's ability to absorb or weigh up a situation through the senses one possesses. I dream in light, dark, atmosphere, sounds, and sensations.
  The dreams that I have are mainly made up of events that I have in reality experienced.
Wally Pepper
(Blind since birth)
Peterborough.

From my experience with my daughter who is blind, the answer appears to be 'yes'. Although the perception of the blind person of such things as monsters, angels, fields etc may be different from our perception, the feeling of sadness or happiness, fear or comfort etc associated with the object is exactly the same.

Faris Bashoo
Camberley, Surrey.

My sister, a visually impaired person since the age of 12 months, says she dreams with the same senses as when she is awake, namely hearing and touch. There is no sight, even in dreams.

Mrs M. Townsend
Wakefield, West Yorkshire.

Blind people dream in much the same way as sighted people. As only four per cent of blind people cannot see anything at all, 96 per cent will have some visual images which may appear in the dreams that they have.

Louisa Fyans
Royal National Institute for the Blind,
London.

CASPARED?

Why is it that when shops have two doors, you always choose the one that is locked?

FACT!

The film *E.T.* was banned to all under elevens in Sweden because the censors thought it showed parents being hostile to their children.

CASPARED?

How come the repairman will never have seen a model quite like yours before?

FACT!

Although the Anglo-American War of 1812 ended with a peace treaty in 1814, its largest battle 'The Battle of New Orleans' actually took place in 1815.

When men get older, why do they lose hair on their head, but gain it in their ears and nose?

Gone soft in the head is what
I'd say,
No firm base for hair to stay,
So down it comes,
And there it goes,
Out of the ears,
And out of the nose!
Mrs B.M. Brennan
Arundel, Sussex.

I am of the belief that as
men get older their nose and
ears are massaged more
regularly than the scalp with
their fingers, thus promoting
growth in the ears and nose
and baldness on their
neglected heads.
Carole Thomas
London.

FACT!

Over £30million is spent on
the purchase of shoe
polish each year in the UK.

Hair in the ears and noses of
older men is not gained as a
consequence of losing the
hair on the head. Ear and
nose hair grows longer and
becomes naturally more
coarse with age and thus
becomes more noticeable.
The amount of hair on the
head is determined quite
separately by the circulatory
system and other conditions
affecting the scalp.
Mr G. Birch
St. Leonards on Sea,
East Sussex.

Men do not lose their hair -
like toenails, it just starts
growing inward. When it
starts appearing in profusion
around the nose and ears,
it's just coming out the other
side.
Jim Bellew
Chipperfield, Herts.

44

Why do our stomachs flutter when we think of something we dread?

When we are afraid or nervous of something our natural reaction is to either run away or stay and fight. To do this, our muscles require more oxygenated blood than usual, so adrenalin is produced. The adrenalin tells our body to send all its blood to the muscles so that they are prepared for the work they have to do. In order to supply the new demand blood is not sent to the stomach and digestive system thus causing the stomach to flutter.
Leanne Long
Dedham, Essex.

When we think of something we dread the nerves to our stomach called the sphlintyc ganglions are stimulated. They cause our stomach to fall by about one centimetre which causes the fluttering sensation.

Thus, to have a 'sinking feeling' is literal as well as metaphorical. The reason for this is to give our lungs and heart more room to work, thus preparing us for action.
Mr J. D. Wallis
Leeds.

CASPARED?

Should modest people describe themselves, by asserting, or by denying their modesty?

FACT!

After being found inside the stomach of a whale after being presumed drowned, seaman James Bartley survived but never returned to sea.

Why is it impossible to tickle yourself?

The main element in a tickle is that of surprise. One can never know exactly where the next tickle is going to 'land', as the contact is initiated by someone else. This not knowing also makes the body especially sensitive to further contact experienced randomly by the subject at the hands of his or her tormentor! Attempts to tickle oneself are thwarted by the body's own inner sensory system. Special sensing devices called proprioceptors continuously inform the brain of the position and movement of all parts of the body in relation to each other. This system effectively pre-empts the surprise element needed for a tickle to have any effect, as the brain has already registered the actual intentions and movements involved, and so brain and body are expecting contact at a specific location.

C.R. Finch
Rhos, Clwyd.

Because we can't reach the parts other ticklers can reach.

Ken Pointon
Tamworth, Staffs.

It is not impossible to tickle yourself, it is just impossible to get the peculiar thrilling sensation that somebody else can.

Mark Brunning
London.

CASPARED?

Why is the national health service not called the national sick service? After all, it is a service for sick people not healthy ones.

CASPARED?

How sick can a parrot really get?

46

Why do women tend to live longer than men?

This is not strictly true. There are instances of cultures in the third world where the roles of men and women are virtually reversed, or at least equal. In these countries the life expectancy also follows a different pattern to our own. The stresses and traumas of our modern society have determined for many years that the male dies earlier. Over the next two or three decades the levels will even out in this country as the more modern female dominates more and more the presently male oriented areas of work, leisure, and sport.
C.E. Clarke
Matlock, Derbyshire.

According to my old maths teacher, women live longer than men because they don't marry women.
Dawna Martin
Canterbury, Kent.

Women live longer than men because man was created first with all his imperfections, whereas woman was created later as the finished, perfect model.
Elizabeth Thorn
Grantham, Lincs.

Girls have less infant mortality than boys.
   Women can stand more pain than men, as in the case of childbirth.
   Women can take greater extremes of temperature.
   Women are more caring about things.
   Women live less stressful lives.
   No wonder they live longer, they're made better than us.
Andrew Procter
Tunbridge Wells, Kent.

Women live longer than men because they must always have the last word.
Lorna Kirkby
Towcester, Northants.

If your teeth are supposed to fall out when your gums rot, why do skeletons have teeth?

During life, gum disease (periodontitis) will destroy the bone in which the tooth sits until it is no longer supported, and falls out. A skeleton that still has teeth has not had gum disease and therefore any bone loss, thus the teeth will stay in place after death.

Roger Brown
Whitechapel, London.

Most of the skeletons the public get to see are archeological, the rest being merely models made for observation of the body. A skeleton which has been dug up will have rotted with the surrounding matter and so when the gums rotted the teeth were encased by mud and so didn't fall out (unlike when you are alive).

Even if the teeth had fallen out when the flesh rotted, they would not fall far and so the archeologists would easily be able to find them and put them back in place. To my knowledge museums and other places where you can see skeletons fill the gaps in the teeth so we always see a toothful bag of bones.

J.A.C. Maines
Glasgow.

When a living being's gums rot the teeth fall out because they are continually dislodged by the movement of the mouth. When a person dies and the gums rot, the teeth stay in place because of the lack of movement that would be needed to knock them out.

David Plank
Poole, Dorset.

They needed teeth to bite the dust in the first place.

Patrick Monario
Wisbech, Cambs.

Do identical twins have the same fingerprints and genetic identity?

At a police open day my identical twin sons volunteered to have their fingerprints taken.
The prints were identical in every way apart from a whorl on the thumb which one had and the other didn't.
Sandra Murrin
Padstow, Cornwall.

Onozygotic or as they are more commonly known 'identical' twins come from the same sperm and ovum. For this reason they are identical in every sense, and therefore will have the same fingerprints and genetic identity.
  Dizygotic or fraternal twins are produced from two different ovum cells and are quite different from one another.
Rakesh Bargota BSc, PhD
King's College, London.

Identical twins are two persons of the same sex who developed from a single fertilised ovum that split into two. They are mirror images of each other in every way, and although their fingerprints will be similar, they too are mirror images. The genetic identity is completely identical.
My father and uncle are identical twins, and because of this, my uncle is my genetic father and his offspring are my cousins and also my genetic half sisters.
Elizabeth Heckman
Rochdale.

If one of the twins is a criminal then I hope not for the sake of the other twin!
Ian English
Bearsden, Glasgow.

What causes the phenomenon of déjà vu?

Some religions believe that we enjoyed a pre-mortal experience before being born where we see snippets of our future life. All we are doing at a time of déjà vu is remembering what we 'viewed' years before.
Colin Smith
Southsea, Hants.

I recently experienced this on and off whilst recovering from the removal of a brain tumour. I was well enough to watch TV and whilst doing so kept remembering the Gulf War pictures, even though I was watching them in many cases 'live', as they were happening.

The cause I believe is simple: the brain registers the message quicker than the eye when the brain is 'racing' for some reason but recovers when the brain slows down to its normal pace.
Mrs A. Kent
St. Ives, Cornwall.

It is suggested that perhaps the person *has* been there before, long ago, perhaps in childhood, and has either forgotten, or 'blocked out' the memory for some reason, but obviously this is only possible in a limited number of cases.

A second possibility is that events in the lifetimes of one's ancestors can be 'recorded' and passed down from one generation to another genetically.

The most plausible theory, however, is that when you have an experience, rather than passing to your short-term memory for 'sorting', sometimes (and for some unknown reason), the experience passes directly to your long-term memory, giving you the impression that you had also had the experience a long time ago, and the memory had been recorded then.
David Barnett
Edgware, Middlesex.

What causes
bags under the eyes?

Without a doubt the answer has to be gravity, age, and husbands.
Mrs Evelyn Turksma
Hemsby, Norfolk.

These are not bags, they are merely desks for tired pupils to lean on.
Roger Webb
Wool, Dorset.

CASPARED?

Why is it that my 90-year-old mother, who is extremely deaf in normal conversation, wakes up from sleep at the slightest sound?

CASPARED?

Why is under a tree the driest place to stand when it rains and yet the wettest place to stand when it has stopped raining?

As people get older, the amount of collagen in the skin decreases. The effect of this is that the elasticity of the skin is reduced and it is particularly noticeable in the areas where connective tissue is thinnest, such as under the eyes.
Roger Brown
Whitechapel, London.

This all came about with the security dictum that bags should not be left unattended. So, we have to keep our eyes on our bags!
Mrs T. Pennel
Southport, Lancashire.

FACT!

Although today his work sells for millions of pounds, during his lifetime it is believed that Vincent Van Gogh sold only one of his paintings.

Bags under the eyes are symptoms of weakened, or even diseased kidneys which cannot efficiently flush out surplus sodium in the system. Our blood plasma, intracellular and extracellular fluids need to maintain constant well-balanced proportions of sodium per fluid volumes. When we consume much more sodium (mainly in salt) than the system can absorb, then a pair of sluggish kidneys cannot flush out all the surplus sodium, and has to retain extra water to dilute the concentration of sodium. When we lie down in our sleep, gravitation draws more body fluid to the hollow eye sockets than to other parts. In the middle years the skin (around the eyes and elsewhere) loosens and becomes less elastic. The result of all the above factors is bags under the eyes and puffiness on the eyelids.

These symptoms are prominent in the morning, after we get out of bed. Some people take the short cut to get rid of their 'eye bags' by resorting to plastic surgery. But the best remedy is to practise a salt-free diet (with lots of potassium-rich fruits, raw vegetables, and freshly prepared juices, which are excellent natural diuretics) to get rid of the symptoms as well as to stop damaging the already weakened kidneys.

N. Nuyen
London W11.

CASPARED?

Why do people do the football pools every week if all they can say when they have won is 'it won't change my life'?

FACT!

One of singer Shirley Bassey's first jobs was wrapping chamber pots.

CASPARED?

What does the bottom of a bird cage taste like, and how does anyone know?

Can hair really turn grey or white overnight?

Despite popular stories to the contrary, it is not possible for hair to turn grey or white literally overnight.

The 'greying' or to be more correct the 'whitening' of hair occurs when the colouring mechanism at the root of each hair ceases to function. Thereafter, each hair so affected grows colourless creating a grey or white appearance.

Failure of the colouring mechanism usually occurs gradually through the ageing process, but can occur suddenly and dramatically as a result of illness, or severe emotional or mental stress. But even then, the speed at which the greying becomes more apparent depends upon the rate at which the new hair grows. Even in extreme cases, this would take several weeks.

Malcolm Cummings
Stourport on Severn, Worcs.

Yes and no! Unless you have an accident with some white paint!

There have however been recorded cases of this happening, the most famous being Marie Antoinette during the French Revolution. She had grey hair (actually a mixture of individual white and darker natural coloured hairs, giving the illusion of grey) on the night before she parted company with her head. As one might imagine, this was a distressing event to anticipate. Stress hormones caused her dark hair to fall out while she slept, leaving only white hairs on her soon to be removed head (the white hairs react differently to hormones, one of the reasons they have already lost their colour). Thus the Queen of France appeared to have gone white overnight, when in fact her white hairs were there all along.

Phillip E. Hatton
Bromley, Kent.

Can people who lipread detect regional accents?

As someone from the south-east I find that the further north a person comes from, the harder they are to understand, with Scottish and Irish almost impossible to 'read'. This is particularly disappointing for me because when I was a hearing person I thought both accents quite lovely.
Mrs J.J. Nichols
Southend on Sea, Essex.

It is possible to lipread some accents. Foreign ones are the worst and are almost impossible unless the person speaking has a very good command of English. Regional accents are a lot easier, more so if you know from the beginning of the conversation where the person comes from.
I have been attending lipreading classes for six years, but it is only within the past 12 months that I have been able to cope with accents.
Mrs Norma Viggers
Stevenage, Herts.

Yes they can. Lipreading depends on the rhythm of speech. This is a valuable aid in understanding what's being said and can vary enormously with different accents.
The lipreader also requires a good view of the face and clear lip movements.
Who said silence is golden?
Mrs Helen Beaumont
Lipreader & Lipreading Teacher.
Letchworth, Herts.

As a deaf adult I can tell you that it is quite possible for lipreaders to detect regional accents. In fact, it is usually the first thing I notice when speaking to somebody new! Lipreaders follow the patterns of speech and, as different accents have different patterns, accents are relatively easy to pick up.
Mrs Karen Over
Enfield, Middlesex.

Why is it that when one person yawns everyone else follows suit?

A yawn is an indication of boredom, therefore if the person you are talking to yawns, you are obviously boring him; if he finds you boring he must be a boring person, so you yawn. Anyone noticing you both yawning would think how boring you both are so he also yawns. The effect is cumulative.
Liandra Chapman
Slough, Berks.

The main reason for this is that they must be reading other, inferior books.
Miss N. Davies
Sidcup, Kent.

It is all part of body language. People who are in tune with one another will often sit in the same position (e.g. right leg crossed over left, head resting on hand etc). When one changes position others, unknowingly, usually follow suit. Watch groups of people to check this theory out - it is true. The same principle applies to yawning.
L. S. Dunning
Shanklin, Isle of Wight.

Yawning is due to lack of oxygen. . . as a person yawns they suck in large amounts of air, which in turn uses up the next person's supply, so they then have to yawn. . . and so it goes on and on.
Jan Carter
Stevenage, Herts.

CASPARED?

If we can't use metal containers in the microwave, why do most of them have stainless steel insides?

CASPARED?

Do frogs ever get a human in their throats?

This illustrates that everybody is affected by suggestion, either directly or indirectly. Indirect suggestion, because it is not recognised by the conscious mind, is much more readily accepted. If you say to someone, 'You are feeling tired', they can choose to disagree with you. But if you yawn the suggestion of tiredness is still there, but being indirect it is not 'censored', and therefore has a stronger influence.

This principle is understood by advertisers, for example when they use a 'story' to sell a product (Oxo and Gold Blend ads are perfect examples). The viewers' attention is on the story, and the impact of the product is greater because they are not consciously aware of it. Subliminal advertising is the most powerful of all. It is not possible to 'censor', and is something of which you have no conscious awareness at all. This has fortunately been banned for this reason.

A.B. King M.I.C.H.
M.G.M.H.
Consultant Hypnotherapist
Waterlooville, Hampshire.

They are probably all listening to the same boring conversation and sharing the same stuffy atmosphere.
D. M. Laidlaw
Arbroath.

CASPARED?

Why do all goalkeepers fall down as soon as a penalty shot is taken against them?

FACT!

In Imperial China, the stealing of a Pekinese dog was a crime that was only punishable by death.

CASPARED?

Why do sheep always eat grass at the side of the road when there is normally a field full of the stuff behind them?

CASPARED?

Why do people never walk or run to keep fit classes?

Does a person who is ambidextrous produce the same handwriting from the left hand as from the right hand?

As somebody who is ambidextrous my writing is very similar if I do mirror writing with my left hand and normal writing with my right. If I write from left to right with both hands the writing becomes very different.
Heather Williams
Brightlingsea, Essex.

If an ambidextrous person wrote with both hands and it looked very different (as is normally the case), it would still be evident to a trained graphologist that the same person had written both samples. This is due to the fact that as the pen is controlled by the brain it will display a combination of conscious and subconscious forces which is a picture of our psychological make-up.
P. A. Johnson
Hastings, East Sussex.

I am ambidextrous and my left hand writing is totally different from that of my right hand. This is due to the positioning of the pen in my hand and the flow of writing from left to right (my right hand pulls the pen, while my left hand pushes the pen).
Mrs E. Sinclair
Morecambe, Lancs.

My old headmaster would write on the board with his left hand, and change over to his right when his hand became tired. There was no deterioration in the quality or speed. This skill, along with his tall, blond good looks, had the whole class totally fascinated.
Rosemary Rowe
Roche, Cornwall.

CHAPTER

THREE

BUT IS IT TRUE?

Is the Latin temperament really more passionate?

I don't think it is a question of a Latin temperament being more passionate, but more of us Brits being less passionate due to our abysmal climate. We have cold drizzly weather for most of the year, and this must surely take its toll in the passion stakes.

This is evident during our holidays to sunnier climes, where the freedom and outgoing nature we nearly all exhibit seems to have always been with us but unfortunately repressed due to colder circumstances.
Shane Friend
Darwen, Lancashire.

A Latin temperament is really more passionate, more volatile, more emotional. Because of all that olive oil and sun the Latin temperament is on constant simmer, ready to reach the boil and even boil over if the occasion seems to warrant it. Gestures, arm-waving, rapid and colourful language (rising passionately of course) is second nature and can come into play over what may seem to us reserved and inhibited islanders, the most insignificant things - which of course they are not.

To the Latin temperament everything is significant, important, worthy of a lively scenario which will be played out, often with great gusto, drama and *passion*.
M Roche
Winchester, Hampshire.

Latin temperament pales besides the Celtic passions of the Welsh. Searing emotions are roused in the female breast by the likes of Anthony Hopkins and Tom Jones. And what of the ladies bewitched by the late lamented Richard Burton, Dylan Thomas and - whisper it - Lloyd George?
Fred Bennett
Llandeilo, Dyfed.

Definitely not! I've had Italian, Spanish and Greek lovers and they have all had one thing in common: their egos. Give me an Englishman anytime.
Rose Cole,
Taunton, Somerset.

Yes it is. They really pull out all the stops for the chase. . . but after . . .!! Fabulous as lovers, hopeless as husbands!! I should know: I married one.
Mrs M. B.
Huddersfield.

Is it true that dead weight is heavier than live weight, and if so, why?

It is not true. Dead and live weights are the same. A 35kg lamb weighs that whether it is dead or alive and a ton of lead weighs the same as a ton of feathers.
F.D. Mason
Berkhamsted, Herts.

The natural muscular tension in a live body means the handling of that body is easier. When a body is unconscious or dead the weight and relaxation of the body make it more difficult to handle, mainly because it is more floppy and thus more awkward to move.
C. Millar
Holywood, Co. Down.

Dead weight is heavier than live weight due to being deflated of air. An example of this can be seen when a boxer weighs in for a contest. They inhale deeply to fill their lungs with air which makes them marginally lighter.
Will Smith
Allestree, Derby.

This is really a stiff question, which I find difficult to undertake. However, it is of grave concern to anybody who works in a funeral parlour, so the answer must rest with them.
Jean Strong
Dundee.

FACT!

One in every two people in the UK wear spectacles or contact lenses.

CASPARED?

If insurance is bliss, why do we always worry about things unknown?

Is there any medical basis for the saying 'feed a cold and starve a fever'?

The saying is not an instruction but a warning, being a truncated version of 'If you feed a cold you'll have to starve a fever'.

This is because the body's natural defence mechanism will use all its resources to fight the cold, but if energy is diverted to digest heavy meals when the system is already sluggish, recovery is slower and the cold could develop into something more severe.

Mrs D.L. Garrard
Greenford, Middlesex.

The expression is a corruption of the correct form which means the exact opposite. If you watch how ill animals function you will see that they tend to eat very little, leaving the body's energy systems free from the work of digestion to concentrate on the defence and healing process. If this is not done the condition may worsen.

Tony Walton
Norwich.

CASPARED?

Why is it that whenever you are trying to find a place on a videotape, you always stop on the adverts?

CASPARED?

Why is it that other people's holiday snaps are incredibly boring, whilst our own are absolutely fascinating?

Is the number 13 really as unlucky as people say?

The number 13 was originally thought to be unlucky by early Christians, since there were 13 guests at the Last Supper before Christ was crucified. More recently, in 1986, surgeons at Cardiff Royal Infirmary decided to compare the number of patients admitted to casualty for each Friday 6th and Friday 13th in the preceding 10 years, to see if people had more accidents on the date. They found that the average number seeking treatment on Friday 6th was 204; on Friday 13th 196. The fear of the number 13 is known as triskaidekaphobia.
Adrienne Wyper, London.

The origin of the reputation of 13 is probably linked to the Last Supper, where 13 were at the table. However, it could also be because the number 13 is the first number in our system that cannot be easily multiplied by a number below it.
Laurie Lowther
Northallerton, North Yorks.

Only in the event of having a size 13 shoe as I do! Apart from the difficulty in obtaining these, manufacturers are averse to include them in the cheaper ranges.
Mr H. Corp
Harlow, Essex.

FACT!

Only twelve people have ever walked on the surface of the Moon.

FACT!

The country of Tonga once produced a postage stamp in the shape of a banana.

Triskaidekaphobia (fear of the number 13) is a plague that affects every superstitious mind in our society. The French don't number their houses 13, the Italians even leave the unfortunate number out of their national lottery and all over Britain and the USA millions of pounds are lost because deals won't be made and people won't go to work on the 13th, especially if it falls on the same day as a Friday.

In Greece, a man by the name of Nick Matounkas, himself the thirteenth child of thirteen, had a hatred of the superstition surrounding the number 13, so much so that he organised an anti-superstition rally where people could go and smash mirrors, throw away lucky horseshoes and the like. Although the event was due to take place on the thirteenth it was unfortunately cancelled as he had a heart attack just before it could take place.
Thomas Hutton
Little Lever, Bolton.

It certainly was for James Joyce, Alexander the Great, Florence Nightingale, H.G. Wells, Dr Samuel Johnson and Richard Wagner who all died on the 13th of a month.
Michael Bull
London

CASPARED?

Why, when you admire somebody's clothes, do they always reply 'Oh I've had it for years'?

CASPARED?

How come you blow on your soup to cool it down, yet you blow on your hands to warm them up?

CASPARED?

Why is it that men are able to lift a toilet seat, but seem to be incapable of putting it down after use?

Can people really die of a broken heart?

In a book on homoeopathic medicine, the author, a doctor, recalled being asked to attend a maid who had suddenly taken to her bed. He prescribed a homoeopathic medicine for depression, but when there was no improvement she was sent to hospital and, under a brilliant physician, underwent every test known to medical science. Although everything was normal, one day she 'turned her face to the wall and died'.

The mystery remained, until among the girl's possessions a letter was found from a policeman telling her he could not continue to see her as he was a married man. The doctor said it was his only experience of someone dying of a broken heart.
Miss S. Clark
Bournemouth, Dorset.

Yes, if they commit suicide to escape the torment.
Kelly Rose
Meopham, Kent.

I believe they can. My grandparents were a devoted couple, rarely apart during their long married life. Unfortunately my grandfather had to spend his last 18 months in hospital. Then within 48 hours of his dying, my grandmother died. It appeared that she had no will to live without him.
Janet Burholt
Dorchester, Dorset.

When I worked for a heart specialist, he had a young man admitted to hospital with a minor heart attack. He was a cheerful type, and making a good recovery until one day his girlfriend visited and told him she was finishing with him. From that moment on he lost the will to live, soon after he had a second heart attack, and died.
Mrs Dianne Webb
London NW8.

It was said that the opera singer Maria Callas died of a broken heart after her longtime friend and lover Aristotle Onassis left her and married Jackie Kennedy. Maria Callas died suddenly of a heart attack, lonely and isolated in her Paris flat.
Anne Phillip
London N9.

Yes, you can die of a broken heart. It isn't because a broken heart is a disease but it is a cause that can lead to stupid things, such as committing suicide. An example of this was Roald Dahl's father. When his daughter died, he caught an illness but felt there was no need to carry on living. It wasn't the broken heart that killed him - but he would maybe have fought the illness if his daughter had been alive.
Miss C. Spence
Appleton, Cheshire.

In western medicine a broken heart is not thought of as an actual medical possibility, and people who are feeling unhappy at the loss of a loved one are encouraged to 'cheer up' and to 'get busy doing something'.

But in Chinese medicine it is understood that sadness caused from a broken heart can result in weakening of the lungs, and lack of interest in food, which result in a general weakness and loss of vitality. This can then lead to a fatal result, if it goes unchecked.

The treatment is to make the sad person angry by some means. Thus begins a cycle of recovery. Later on some sympathy will then be helpful, when the person's appetite returns.
S. MacNamara
London W11.

CASPARED?

If moths like light so much why don't they come out during the day?

CASPARED?

Why is it that when you have lost something people always say 'where did you put it last'?

67

Do cats really have nine lives?

No, but their agility enables them to get out of perilous situations more than other animals. High speed photography has shown that when a cat falls, even from an upside down position, it somehow manages to turn in the air and land on its feet which are padded to sustain the impact almost like built-in shock absorbers. Also in Egypt over 3000 years ago cat killing was punishable by death. With such protection, cats were unlikely to die prematurely.
David Shepherd
London.

Cats don't really have nine lives. This is derived from the whip called the Cat-o-Nine tails that was used on ships, etc. As the whip had nine 'tails' it didn't matter if one broke as there were eight remaining. Hence 'the cat had nine lives'.
Alan Gibson
Huddersfield, W. Yorkshire.

Perhaps this idea originates from Thomas Gray's poem, 'A favourite cat drowned in a tub of goldfishes':

Eight times emerging from
  the flood
She mewed to every watery
  God
Some speedy aid to send:-
No dolphin came, no Nereid
  stirr'd
No cruel Tom nor Susan
  heard -
A favourite has no friend!
George Fox
Bournemouth, Dorset.

This dates back to mediaeval times when cats were thought to be the servants of witches. These cats were hunted down and killed but it was thought that the witch could reincarnate the cat's soul, and so bring it back from the dead, up to nine times. If this is true then cat's really do have nine lives.
P. Rossiter
Widnes, Cheshire.

If they can get away with it cats would have more; however, they must stay content with nine - birds, mice, hamsters, voles, rats, shrews, goldfish, moles and gerbils.
F. E. Evans
Llanybyter, Dyfed.

As there is a time-honoured practice of drowning kittens at birth, the answer is probably No!
William McCrea
Preston, Lancashire.

Cats are so skilled and nimble that they avoid what looks like certain death. This may be one reason why they are regarded as being lucky. It is that luckiness which gives the clue to the number nine. Nine was once known as a holy number, and so, as superstition follows religious decline, became a lucky number.
Father Terence McCann
Manchester.

Why does a red sky in the morning indicate good weather, yet a red sky in the morning is an omen of rain?

The explanation for this phenomenon is a combination of the structure of 'light', atmospheric conditions, and the rotation of the world.

When the sun is low in the sky, as at daybreak or sunset, the lightwaves have to travel through a thicker band of atmosphere than if it were directly overhead. This has a greater filtering effect and as such most colours in the spectrum are either absorbed or deflected, leaving only the most robust red waves to reach the earth. Thus we can enjoy the glorious sunsets and sunrises.

However, the intensity of illumination is dependent on the incidence of dry dust particles in the upper atmosphere. Now, as all weather systems travel west to east, when the sun sets on an evening in the west it is obviously illuminating a dry atmosphere which is yet to arrive.

Conversely, as the sun rises in the east, and therefore illuminates the eastern skyline the 'red sky in the morning' is a sign that the dry dust must have passed by, and wetter, stormier weather is just around the corner.

Very simple, but one of the most reliable systems of weather forecasting.
M. Magowan
Sunderland.

FACT!

If you stood on Tower Bridge and watched the passing of the River Thames for a whole year you would still not see as much water as passes down the River Amazon in only one day.

70

Is John Smith really Britain's most common name?

If hotel registers are anything to go by - yes!
Mrs A. Jones
Coventry.

John Smith is indeed Britain's most common name, closely followed by John Williams and John Taylor. In America, John Smith has a society devoted solely to his welfare.

'Smith' originally meant a foundryman or metalworker, as in Blacksmith, Ironsmith, Coppersmith and so on. It evolved into a catchall term like 'wright', meaning anyone who worked with his hands.

In pre-Industrial Revolution Britain, when the majority of families were peasant class, illiterate and named after their profession or place of residence, any Cartwright, Wainwright, Cooper or other artisan who could not spell his own name could conveniently and legitimately call himself 'Smith'.

'John' is one of those short, sweet, virtually phonetic Biblical names that transcends fashion by virtue of its simplicity and plainness. Wayne and Darren, River and Keanu come and go but John lives on forever.
Tessa Kamara
Ealing, London.

The most recent published count showed 659,050 nationally insured Smiths in Great Britain, of whom 10,102 were plain John Smith and another 19,502 were John (plus one or more middle names) Smith. Including uninsured persons, there were over 800,000 Smiths in England and Wales alone, of whom 81,493 were called A. Smith.
H. Hodson
Birmingham.

What really is the oldest profession?

The answer is flint-knapping - the manufacture of fist axes, spear heads, and other similar chopping tools from raw flint, dated from two and a half million years ago in Ethiopia, West Africa. Other professions such as agriculture, fishing, animal husbandry, trading in amber, grave robbing, and prostitution are incomparably younger.
Bill Robinson
South Ruislip, Middlesex.

CASPARED?

Why is it that vices are more habit forming than virtues?

CASPARED?

Why did kamikaze pilots wear crash helmets?

The oldest profession is that of advertising. In the Book of Genesis we read that Adam and Eve were allowed to eat the fruit of all the trees in the Garden of Eden, except for one tree, and if they ate the fruit of that one, they would die. 'But the serpent said to the woman, "You will not die. . . you will be like God. . ."' That was the world's first advertisement - and a lie. Afterwards of course came the buckpassing.
J. C. Thompson
Lincoln.

The oldest profession is that of gardener according to the Bible. In Genesis 3:15, following the account of the creation of Adam, we read, 'And the Lord God took the man and put him into the Garden of Eden to dress it and to keep it'.
Alison J. Perry
Harefield, Middlesex.

It is rumoured that prostitution is the oldest profession but I am of the opinion that the oldest profession is actually begging - after all, someone had to ask for it didn't they?
Julia McKie
Warrington, Cheshire.

According to the Old Testament, the first occupation and, presumably therefore, the first profession practised by mankind was that of fruitpicker.
George Hume
Swinton, Manchester.

Horticulturalists will say that their profession came first as Adam worked in the Garden of Eden. Architects will say that their profession came first as God created the Garden of Eden from out of the Chaos. The truth is that Politicians came first because they created the Chaos in the first place.
David J. Foster
Wallsall.

FACT!

The railway locomotive was invented nearly 35 years before the first bicycle.

FACT!

Swastikas have been discovered as symbols used by North and South American Indian tribes and have been discovered on Byzantine buildings, Celtic monuments, Greek coins, and Buddhist inscriptions.

FACT!

Mozart wrote his symphonies Nos. 39, 40, and 41 in the space of 42 days.

FACT!

The first photograph of the Moon was taken on 2 January 1840 by Dr J.W. Draper of New York.

FACT!

Over 200,000 tonnes of washing up liquid is poured down the sinks of British households each year.

Does life really begin at forty?

I'm 43 and most of my friends are of a similar age. After asking round I can conclusively say we are all still waiting.
Janet Hillman
Chesterfield.

The expression 'life begins at forty', originates from Roman times when it was considered an honour for a family to enlist their daughter on her tenth birthday into the Temple of Vesta. The girl would remain in the temple for the next 30 years and live as a vestal virgin: a simple life of prayer, abstinence and charity work. Even to see a man was forbidden and would result in expulsion.

On her fortieth birthday the unfortunate (or fortunate) lady would be released, and undoubtedly began her new life as soon as possible. It seems rather ironic that in Roman times women considered 'life' to be the freedom to pursue men while in modern times it is increasingly considered to be freedom not to. One suspects that the ancient tradition of Vesta would bring disgrace to a modern family but that a temple for the over forties would be quite acceptable.
Janet Beveridge
Dulverton, Somerset.

The saying comes from the French, who say themselves, that we spend twenty years growing, twenty years working, and twenty years living. This probably dates back to a time when the life expectancy in France was only 60 years or so.
Janice Grahame.
Dublin.

Yes life does begin at forty - forty weeks after conception.
Mrs Linda Ogden
Chadderton, Lancs.

No, but it makes us live in hope for another forty.
Lesley Boyd
Bracknell, Berkshire.

Does thunder
turn milk sour?

Milk does not go sour purely as a result of thunder. It is simply that the climatic conditions that give rise to thundery weather also provide the perfect environment for bacteria to thrive in unrefrigerated milk.

The very same effect occurs in other foodstuffs although in some cases it is not always noticeable.

Mr A.G. Atkinson
Sunderland.

All farmers know that the weather can be predicted from the behaviour of animals in fields. On sensing thunder, cows normally gallop for shelter, and this churns up the milk inside their udders. Therefore, it is curdled when they come to be milked.

Mrs Ellen Conlon
Co Armagh, N. Ireland.

Yes, thunder does turn milk sour.

When breastfeeding my baby son many years ago he became fractious and refused to feed during thunderstorms.

Nothing else affected his appetite.

Mrs D.M. Mullineux
Eastbourne, East Sussex.

Yes. As a child living on a farm during the 1940's, I remember after thunderstorms, the milk was always sour, not just slightly turned, but thick. 'Thick as a liver' was the local expression.

Milk nowadays is different, pasteurised and refrigerated, bearing little resemblance to that natural product I am talking about. But given the right conditions, such as a power cut, thunder would still turn it sour.

Mrs K. Wilson
County Tyrone.

Can people ever forget how to ride a bike?

Probably not. This is because of kinaesthetic memories. These reinforce verbal and visual memories and allow people to recall spatial and muscular skills better and longer than any other memories. These memories are stored deep within the brain and are evident in people who have not ridden a bike in 20, 40, even 60 years but can still get safely back in the saddle.
P. Foster
Eastbourne, East Sussex.

Yes they can!
John Harwood
Ward 2
(Accident and Emergency)
Leamington Spa Hospital.

I would suggest that people never forget how to ride a bike, though some do forget how to stay upright on it.
David Smulovitch
Edgware, Middlesex.

No, but they can forget where their bike is!
Sarah Major
Worksop, Notts.

CHAPTER

FOUR

VIVE LA DIFFERENCE!

Why are the openings of men's trousers referred to as flies?

The openings of men's trousers are called flies because this is actually an anagram of files. And files, as we all know are designed to keep things in good order, awaiting future reference.
Joan Jarvis
Warrington, Cheshire.

Men's trousers are referred to as flies because they were invented by a swot.
A. Kruse
Bury St Edmunds, Suffolk.

This is yet another legacy of the British maritime heritage. The term fly is applied to the free or loose end of ropes, flags, sails, and to tent flaps. When men's breeches required closing by loose flaps of material, two to make the closure and one to cover the join discreetly, it was natural to refer to them as flies.
D.A. Twiss
East Grinstead, Sussex.

The opening of men's trousers are called flies, but factually this is wrong. The fly is the flap which covers the zip or buttons to neaten the appearance.

To add to this the word fly is also the name given to the curtain or board which covers the front of the lights at the top and sides of a stage so the audience does not see them.

Dazzling information.
Mrs B.A. Wilkinson
Bradford, West Yorkshire.

They ain't. The one at the front is called 'fly' and those at the side are called pockets.
Robert Arthur
Bideford, Devon.

The opening of men's trousers are referred to as flies because they go Z.Z.Z.Z.Z.Z.Z.Zip when you close them.
Gail White
Shirley, Southampton.

79

Why do bras fasten at the back when it would seem more sensible for them to fasten at the front?

This appears to be a convention developed from traditional corsetry. Front openings were first designed for sportswear about 1910 by an American manufacturer, Menzies. In the 1920's a few 'front loading' designs were also seen in fashionable lingerie. However, they are more traditionally used for maternity and sportswear. It is likely that back fastenings have persisted because there is more room for fine adjustment at the back, i.e. several rows of hooks and eyes, whereas at the front there is room for just one hook.

Avril Hart
Victoria and Albert Museum
London.

In this nuclear age I thought they fastened at the back to stop fall out.

John Vance
Fife.

This is a deliberate design policy which has been stringently adhered to for many years by the foundation garment industry. The contortions involved in trying to fasten a back fastening bra are very similar to the exercises designed to increase muscle tone and consequently to increase the size of the bust measurement. This in turn leads to higher sales of more expensive larger sized bras. Simple!

Susan Ormond
Burghfield Common,
Reading.

To those of us with a DD cup the answer is obvious. There is too much underwire metal cantilevering the edifice up at the front already without adding to it by an assortment of hooks and eyes.

Ann Carlton
London.

A back fastening bra can have two or more rows of eyes to allow for a more exact fitting and to allow for any stretching of fabric through continued usage. After all, while bra sizes increase in two inch jumps, women's sizes do not!

Also, apart from the single fastening possible on a plunge-front bra, any deeper fastening would look clumsy and destroy the smooth line at the front.

June Kenton
London.

Bras fasten at the back because it is almost impossible to scoop up the required contents and hold them still while fastening the bra at the front. Any grandmother who has worn what was called a 'Nursing Bra' (front fastening) thirty-odd years ago knows about this problem. The only way to encase the entire female protrusions is to bend forward slightly, allow them to fall into the cups and pull the bra backwards. This avoids escapes, painful pinching and other hazards.

Eileen Denham
Kent.

Bras fasten at the back because at one time all ladies would have been dressed by a maid. It would not have been seemly for the unfortunate girl to be fastening hooks in her mistress's cleavage. Sadly nowadays bras do not come with their own ladies' maid.

Helen Bailey
Northwich, Cheshire.

FACT!

The Jeep, the vehicle developed during World War Two got its name from it's initials, GPV, which stood for General Purpose Vehicle.

FACT!

The first person ever to be put to death in the electric chair, murderer William Kemmler, took eight minutes to die.

FACT!

The first ever car to be stolen was a Peugeot in 1896. The thief was eventually caught.

Why do women cross their arms when they take off a jumper and yet men tug at the neck?

After discussing this phenomenon at the office where I work I have discovered that there are in fact three methods of removal. The last of these (and unmentioned in the question) seems to be favoured by the more 'delicate' people, and consists of the arms being gently removed from the jumper first, followed by a caring lift of the garment over the head.

Going back to the question it seems that in the main it is the men who, traditionally being the more aggressive, are the exponents of the tug it over class of jumper removal. The women, who by my reckoning are generally more caring, try to keep the shape of their clothes and their physique with a more dignified and serene crossover technique.

I don't know if this has answered your question but thank you for asking it anyway as my investigations led to a good time being had by all, and I think I've got the basis for a great new boardgame for adults.
*Blodwyn Maddog
Penrhiwceibr,
Mid Glamorgan.*

Women are unable to tug at the neck without causing severe discomfort to their upper regions. Men can use both methods but seemingly prefer the more awkward of the two.
*Christopher Brown
Aylesbury, Bucks.*

The answer is a simple matter of hair styles. No woman would ruin her hair by dragging a jumper over it, while with most men this isn't so important.
*C. M. Wright
Higher Broughton, Salford.*

Where does the term 'wally' originate and does it have a female equivalent?

Wally was a dog which strayed from its owner at the original Glastonbury Fayre Festival in the late 1960's. As its owner wandered around calling its name, the crowd took up the cry 'wally' whilst waiting for the next band to tune up.
This was so enjoyable that over the next few years, the habit of calling 'wally' caught on at any concert where there was a lull in the proceedings (a bit like today's Mexican wave). Gradually the term 'wally' became transferred to anybody who seemed lost or was perceived as not quite in tune with the proceedings.
Gordon Taylor
Alvaston, Derby.

The term wally originates from the weedy character Walter in the Dennis the Menace cartoon in the Beano.
Michael Nulty
March, Cambs.

The word wally originates from the northern slang word given to the last gherkin in a large jar at a chipshop.
As for the female equivalent, it has been suggested that 'wallette' is appropriate, but this is perhaps too strong a reminder of where your money goes when involving yourself with a female.
Ivan Miller
Derby.

The term derives from the adjective 'wall-eyed', meaning to have a staring or blank expression. Such a person was assumed to be dim-witted and was called a 'wall-eye', later contracted to 'wally'.
The term is exclusive to men who act in a foolish or unwise fashion. There is no female equivalent as women are not known to behave in this way.
Anne Britten
St. Albans, Herts.

Why do English ties have stripes that go down from the left yet American ties go down from the right?

The format of the stripes is simply answered by the fact that Americans do not have our heraldic tradition. A stripe on a coat of arms going down from the right would indicate a bastard line in genealogy.

As most of our ties go down from the left, I guess that the British don't wish to be seen being from the wrong side of the covers.

William Guy
Solihull, West Midlands.

Stripes first appeared in 1880. They were instigated by the clubs (schools, Universities), who needed something less formal for their members to wear at weekends in the country.

All stripes were diagonal and sported the club's colours. Ties were cut on the bias for strength to avoid distortion. In America the stripes go from high right to low left, the opposite to England. This is purely for economics, British cloth is cut one layer at a time, whereas the Americans cut theirs in bulk, wrong side down and then reverse it.

Mrs Wendy Dunn
Oldham, Lancashire.

The tie industry in the United States cut their ties with the pattern of the cloth face down, and this results in the stripes running from high right to low left. Ties in Britain are cut with the design face up, possibly so the design can be seen, resulting in a high left to a low right stripe. There are exceptions and the RAF and Royal Marines ties are but two of many official ties which are cut in the 'American way'.

Jack Griffiths
Worthing, West Sussex.

84

Why do women button right over left and men button left over right?

The fact that a man's clothing buttons left over right and women's clothing vice versa, stems from the Georgian and Victorian dressing practices of the gentry of those times.

Men would receive their clothing from a butler and dress themselves. Having buttons on the right hand side makes this operation simpler for right-handed persons. On the other hand, ladies would be dressed by a handmaid, for whom it would have been easier to have the buttons on the opposite side.
Gary Gleghorn
Cambridge.

So they can get at each other on the back row of the cinema!
R. Porter
Liverpool.

Many years back, before buttons, buggies and 'working mothers', women usually had babies with them. Babe was carried in the crook of her left arm, leaving her right hand free for domestic chores; and to hold her cloak around the baby; hence, right over left. Man, meanwhile, was out being the defender; sword on his right hip. His (right) swordarm had to to be free, and ready for action; hence, his left arm was used to wrap his cape around himself (and his precious right arm); hence, left over right.
Hilma Miles
Fareham, Hampshire.

CASPARED?

Why do slugs never eat the weeds?

Which are better for the average man: Boxer Shorts or Y-Fronts?

Sperm require a lower temperature than that of the body (37°C) to mature, and it is for this reason that testicles are in a cooler area outside the main body. Y-Fronts push the testicles towards the body where the temperature is higher, thus fewer sperm mature. Boxer shorts provide less restriction, allowing the testicles to resume their natural 'cooler' position, keeping the sperm mature and increasing a man's fertility.
A. Tucker
Fairwater, Cardiff.

First you have to decide on what is the average man. Is he tall, short, fat, thin, young or old. Is he a clerical worker, manual worker, fireman, fisherman, policeman or postman etc etc. Now, when you have sorted out your average man, you go to the other part of your question. 'Better for what!!' Drinking in, driving in, running in, resting in. Maybe bowling in or boxing in, walking in or waiting in. As a famous member of the Brains Trust once said 'It all depends'. And, if you still can't decide then choose 'long-johns'. (That's another question.)
Mr J. Williams
Ruislip, Middlesex.

To take this argument to its logical conclusion, might I suggest that the healthiest approach of all is to abandon both and wear a kilt instead!
John A. C. McFarlane
Insch, Aberdeenshire.

I think that boxer shorts are better than Y-fronts for the average man. They are ideal for dancing - plenty of ballroom.
M Webb
Newport, Gwent.

In the 1960's the 'Y' front emblem was used by the Ban the Bomb campaign with a warning 'Beware of Fall Out'. Those people labelled as 'drop outs' were considered to be socially unacceptable. Now it seems the containment issue has gone full circle or circles as we are advised not to give them a hoist to keep them moist but wear boxers to surround them with fresh air. Do we therefore answer the wrangle by letting them dangle? Perhaps we should consult the authority who carries the real weight around here. Richard, it's over or under to you.

P. J. Ford
Hatfield, Hertfordshire.

Research shows that 73 per cent of all males taken into a hospital following a road traffic accident are in fact wearing Y-fronts.

That proves that not only are boxers better for you, but are also a leap forward in road safety.

Steve Sumner
Blackpool, Lancs.

My average man says boxers are best!

Julie Bloom
Hull.

Boxer shorts are better for swinging bachelors than wife runts.

Alan Lewis
High Wycombe, Bucks.

Why do you never see women serving in Indian restaurants?

Many of the first 'Indian' restaurants in Britain were begun by men coming from what used to be east Pakistan, and especially one particular area of it, Sylhet. These men were predominantly Muslim. Originally they came to this country without their wives, working in a variety of industries, mills etc. So to begin with most of the restaurant staff would have been male.

Later, when their wives were able to join them, it would have been unthinkable for a Muslim woman to have mixed with or served strangers (men).
Yvonne Malik
Rhodes, Manchester.

Indian women are so busy serving their husbands, they do not have time to serve anyone else!
D. R. Radia
London.

With regard to your question I feel I must inform you that you can see a woman working as a waitress. She works in the 'Jewel in the Crown', in the High Street, Moseley and to my knowledge has been there several years.
Miss J.E. Thomas
Edgbaston, Birmingham.

There are different grounds for this, corresponding to the religious bent of the proprietors.

It is against the laws of Islam for women to work away from the home, and in the case of the Hindu owned establishments women are regarded as unclean during their menstrual periods, which naturally affects their usefulness as waitresses.
Frederic Mullally
Former Editor,
Sunday Standard, Bombay.

Why are beauty spots so called?

Beauty spots are actually moles. They are given their name from the 17th century custom of covering any facial blemish such as pox marks or scars.

The covering was normally made of velvet and cut into different shapes and then stuck on the face.

The fashion for beauty spots became very popular to such an extent that people who had real facial moles were seen as being especially good looking.

The tradition has continued and some facial marks and moles are still regarded as enhancing the looks of an individual.

This is perhaps one of the nicer ways of dealing with human difference and shows that something that might have been regarded as ugly, when taken from a positive view can be seen as something wonderful.
Donna Pickering
Oldham, Lancs.

A beauty spot is so called because it is a place where it is beautifully easy to leave a shopping trolley rather than take it back to the supermarket.
Mrs T. Murphy
Dorchester, Dorset.

As any mother or father will know, one of the worst things that can happen to a child is to be criticised for any physical flaw they may have. When a child is crying because other children are mocking a facial mole it is only natural that a parent would comfort the child with the knowledge that a facial blemish is not actually a bad thing but instead a sign of beauty.

Over the years this has continued until we now have a situation where a blemish is not actually a blemish any more but instead is actually regarded as a beautiful spot.
Doreen Ravenscroft
Handforth, Cheshire.

Why and when did men start to shave?

Primitive razors have been unearthed in ancient graves, as early man discovered that a beard could easily be grasped by an enemy. It is recorded that Alexander the Great (356-323BC) ordered his soldiers to shave before battle.

The earliest razors were made of flint or sharpened sea shells until the bronze age, when they were made of bronze naturally.
Colin Blomeley
Liskeard, Cornwall.

Shaving became imperative when Og discovered flint and set fire to his face!
D. Jupitus
Stanford-le-Hope, Essex.

I can't speak for other men, but for me it was because I needed to at 7.50 this morning.
Brian Smith,
Brighton.

Shaving implements, such as sharpened flints, clam shells and shark's teeth have been recognised on prehistoric cave drawings. The idea of using flints has passed through the generations to some very primitive, cut-off tribes of today. In Egyptian tombs, from around the 4th millennium BC, solid gold and copper razors have been excavated. The Roman historian, Livy, recorded that razors were first brought to Rome by Lucius Tarquinus Priseus, legendary King of Rome, in the 6th century BC; although shaving did not become customary until the 5th century BC. The most likely reasons for starting to shave were simply to feel clean, comfortable and to look good.
C. Ridings
Bury, Lancashire.

When women started to complain.
J. F. Norris
Chipping, Preston.

Why do men's bicycles have crossbars?

This is in fact a question that should be asked in reverse and should be, why don't women's bicycles have a crossbar?

Original bicycles built with a crossbar were rode nearly always by menfolk, the crossbar being a natural way to stabilise the supports coming vertically up from its wheels.

When the time arrived for it to be socially acceptable for women to ride bicycles, the crossbar was repositioned on a downward slant to give dual tubes. This retained the bicycle's rigidity and was accepted as being strong enough to take the lighter weight of the smaller bodied female. At the same time this new design removed the embarrassment of having a lady throw her leg over the saddle.

Norman Turner
Royton, Oldham.

Men's bicycles have crossbars because they are part of the best construction for a cycle frame. The triangular shape makes for a more rigid frame.

Women's bicycles have an open frame because it is easier and more elegant for a woman wearing a skirt to mount the machine by stepping through the frame rather than having to cock a leg over the saddle.

In these days of unisex clothing both sets of cycling enthusiasts ride the more efficient bicycles with crossbars.

Mrs C. Derbyshire
Congleton, Cheshire.

Men's bicycles were invented with crossbars by a woman as yet another way of keeping men on their toes.

Marion Armstrong
Keighley, West Yorkshire.

Why are
men's umbrellas
larger than women's?

I could be flippant and say that it's to cover their big heads. But it is in reality a throwback to the days of wide hooped skirts and pale complexions. A lady's parasol was only large enough to prevent her face from being scorched by the sun, thus ruining her complexion. It was her escort's duty, therefore, to supply ample covering for the rest of her, should it rain.
Miss I.G. Harvey
Bishopton, Renfrewshire.

One has to think many years ago when London and other large cities were fogbound and grimy: typical Sherlock Holmes weather.

Gentlemen had capes and canes, often with heavy knobs to drive off thugs, urchins and stray dogs. The length of the cane suited men's average size.
As umbrellas came, the length remained the same.

To fit a small umbrella to an average man's 'stick' would have looked rather silly, half way down the stem.

The other reason is top hats. They would have been very difficult to cover with a small brolly.
L. Beddoe
Ruthin, Clwyd.

Women are dangerous enough with umbrellas, liable to poke people's eyes, without them being any bigger. Besides they wouldn't be able to carry the burden of the extra weight.
Paul Weedon
Wotton Under Edge,
Gloucestershire.

Men's umbrellas are larger because most men are taller than women, thus with most rain falling at an angle a small umbrella would result in men getting wet feet.
Paul Wells
Holbury, Hants.

CHAPTER

FIVE

WHERE DID THAT
COME FROM?

Why do calendars begin the week with a Sunday?

Quite simply, the calendars are correct!

To this day, Hebrew has no names for weekdays (except the Sabbath - 'Shabat') only numbers i.e. 'The First Day', 'The Second Day' and so on. Likewise Greek, 'The Second Day', through 'The Fifth Day' are so called; only Friday, Saturday and Sunday are named respectively 'The Day of Preparation', 'The Sabbath' and 'The Lord's Day'. Languages as diverse as Russian and Portuguese still call the seventh day 'The Sabbath'. What we call Sunday is still the First Day of the Week, but was established as the Christian day of worship during the reign of the Roman Emperor Constantine in the 4th century for several reasons. Firstly, his family deity, prior to conversion, was 'Sol Invictus', the Invincible Sun, whose day of worship still bears his name.

Secondly, Sun-worship was widespread in the Empire, and so assimilating it aided conversion to the early Roman church.

Thirdly, as the Jews were suffering increasing persecution, it served the Church to abandon the early Christian Sabbath and with it any danger of being perceived as a sect of Judaism. Nonetheless, this adopted tradition never altered the fact that the week *ends* on the Sabbath and *starts* on Sunday.
Mr G. A. McGregor
Glasgow.

So that we can have our rest of the week first. Followed, of course, by the rest of the week.
Mrs L. Brown
Sidcup, Kent.

It's due to British Rail lore. Having achieved the notion of standardtime in the last century with trains running a good 24 hours late, Sunday schedules were moved to Mondays to cancel delays.
William T. Guy
Knowle, Solihull.

Why is a kiss written as a cross?

A kiss is written as a cross because lovers would literally seal their billets-doux with a kiss. The X marks the spot where lips met with paper! The recipient would presumably kiss the X knowing that their sweetheart's lips had touched the same spot.
Miss E. Bax
Margate, Kent.

A kiss is written as a cross because it looks like two sets of lips joining for a kiss. The first half is one set of lips, the other half is another set of lips.
Erica Slakhorst
Ashford, Middlesex.

FACT!

Many American Indian tribes believed that the earth was actually the back of a massive turtle which floated in the sea.

This practice began in the middle ages, when many people were unable to write. If they had to sign something, they would put a cross on the paper. As it was the sign of St. Andrew it indicated that they had signed in good faith. As a further sign of sincerity, they would then kiss the cross they had written.
Miss Joanne Seal
Andover, Hants.

The ancient Norse alphabet consists of twenty four symbols or Runes. One of these was the cross, which represented a gift or partnership and was particularly relevant to romance, relationships and marriage. Therefore the cross has come down from Viking times as a sign indicating affection - hence the Kiss.
Ian Shaughnessy
Buckley, Clwyd.

Why do the British drive on the left?

The reason is that in the very early days a traveller never knew whether the next person he met on the road would be a friend or foe, so, as the majority of people were right handed, he would veer to the left in order to meet the other with his right hand ready to defend himself. Thus it became customary to keep to the left of the lane, road or track. This was common practice throughout Europe and Asia.

Until Napoleonic times it was customary for troops in battle to be drawn up in lines facing each other and advance, engage in battle, then on the order of the commander, wheel left and attack the enemy flank. In one important battle Napoleon, to the surprise of the enemy, wheeled his men to the right and won an outstanding victory. To celebrate this victory Napoleon decreed that all Frenchmen would walk and ride on the right hand side of the road.

As Napoleon had conquered much of Europe it soon became customary for all mainland Europe to keep to the right, with the exception of Sweden.

Great Britain, unaffected by Napoleon's decrees, continued to move on the left, as do many countries which were once under Britain's influence such as Australia, India, Burma etc.

V.G.N. Rose
Southampton, Hants.

To put it quite simply it is because we have and display superior intelligence.
A left hand drive vehicle has the accelerator towards the centre of the car in a position which, in many cars, can be easily and dangerously touched by the front passenger. A right hand drive has the accelerator tucked up in the right hand corner of the vehicle, well away from all passengers.
In top gear the lever of a left hand drive car is nearest to

the passenger whereas in a right hand drive car the gear lever, when in top gear, is where it should be, beside the driver.

Left is, in any case, the natural side on which to drive. Athletic track events are run anti-clockwise i.e. the nearest side lane is on the left. Similarly, with motor cycle speedway, cycle sprint racing and ice speed skating the nearside is on the left. The port (home) side of a vessel is on the left. Aircraft pass each other to the left. Greyhounds run with the nearest track on the left.

Even ballroom dancers travel anti-clockwise. There is no good reason to drive on the right hand side, and the British, quite correctly, appreciate this.
Ken Randall
(writing from the left)
Westcliff on Sea, Essex.

We don't drive on the right because we would probably get arrested.

Flippancy apart, the main reason we don't drive on the right is due to the enormous cost in making the change.
P. Sutton
Brighton.

Is the use of applause a universal signification of approval or do some other cultures use other kinds of gesture?

If you attended a theatrical production for the deaf community, you would probably see people waving their hands in the air, as this is the sign language equivalent of clapping.
Jane Thomas
Barry, South Glamorgan.

A 'salaam' (palm facing upwards), accompanied by cries of 'vah-vah', is an expression of approval at an Urdu concert (Quavvali), to which the singer responds likewise with an 'Irshad'. The showering of coins and flowers can be seen at the end of many theatrical performances here in the West as a common sign of approval, and there are many others such as shouts of 'Bravo' etc.
Bobby Brown
Southampton.

There are various other alternatives which include banging a spoon on a plate as in the army, whistling, as with audiences, and jumping up and down by children. There are also shouting, stamping, nodding used by various cultures and anybody who has been to Spain will have heard Encore and Olé.
It is also applicable to add heavy breathing!
Mrs I. R. Marcus
London.

In Iceland we attended an amateur production and were surprised to be chastised by the audience for showing our approval in the 'usual' way. Apparently in this culture, a series of ridiculous chants of varying intensity are the 'norm'.
Nick McDowell
Belfast.

Is an orange called an orange because it's an orange, or was the colour orange named after the fruit?

Introduced by the Arabs in about the 9th century to south-western Asia, the fruit was called in Arabic *Naranj*. From this most Europeans have derived their name for the fruit such as the Italian *arancia* (originally narancia) and Spanish *naranja*. Etymologically it seems that the N was dropped due to confusion with the indefinite article (una, une), equivalent to an English slip from a 'norange' to an 'orange'. (A contrary example is a 'newt' which was originally an 'ewt'). Similarly the vowel seems to have been confused with the French *or* (gold). Indeed in the Middle Ages the orange was often called the *pomme d'or* (gold apple) and it is from the French that the English name derives.
Mr G.A. McGregor
Glasgow.

The word orange comes from the Arabic and refers to the colour of the sand and rocks in North Africa. When the Arab traders visited China around the 15th century, they brought back the fruit and plants for cultivation. Because the rind of the orange, yellowish-red, resembled the sand and rocks it was called 'Naranj' which Europeans pronounce as orange.
Mr A. Greening
Nottingham.

FACT!

The film
Gone with the Wind
started filming before the
role of Scarlett O'Hara had
even been cast.

Why do we put stamps on the top right hand corner of envelopes?

On 7 May 1840, the Secretary of the General Post Office issued a notice to the public requesting that stamps be placed on the top right hand corner of the front of letters 'due to the rapidity with which the duty must be performed'. This referred to the post officer responsible for cancelling stamps with a hand impression, whose job was made easier by having all the stamps in the same position on the envelope.
Dave Rayner
Canterbury, Kent.

Since the introduction of the first postage stamp (the penny black) in 1840, the tradition has evolved of placing the stamp on the top right hand corner of the envelope. Nobody knows why this first began but it is probably due to the fact that most people are right handed.

A century and a half later this tradition still continues; however today the reason is more practical and is simply related to aiding a more efficient sorting system.
Merle Adam,
Belsize Park, London.

The reason we put postage stamps in the right hand corner of envelopes is to enable the postman and the public to write cryptic messages to each other in the left hand corner (FRAGILE, HANDLE WITH CARE, etc).

One such example occurred in Hampstead when an irate woman came in the Post Office brandishing a brown envelope. In the left hand corner, written in red was 'Photos - do not bend'. Alongside it the postman had written 'Oh yes they do' and bent it in half and stuffed it through her letterbox!
Robert Peacock
Edgware, Middlesex.

This is due to developments throughout the years of systems that have vastly improved the speed of our postal service.

Its origins can be traced back to the end of the 15th century. During the reign of Charles II, a Colonel Henry Bishop was appointed Post Master General. He made it his responsibility to reduce the number of complaints concerning none or late delivery of mail. Thus he decreed that each letter should be embossed with an impression to contain the date in the month that it was offered for posting.

In 1730 it was the turn of Rowland Hill to revolutionise the postal system once more. He realised that the costs of the service were so cumbersome that any meaningful calculations of tariff were becoming impossible to enforce. He therefore suggested that all letters should be pre-paid by means of attaching a small piece of paper to signify the correct fees had been paid. Thus was born the adhesive stamp of which the penny black was the first and of course the most famous. By combining Colonel Bishop's block stamp and Rowland Hill's adhesive paper the system of cancelling mail became common. It became customary to place the stamp in the top right hand corner to facilitate quick and easy cancellation by the majority of postmasters who were in the main right handed.

Of course, nowadays, we have mechanised cancellation and this has made it more important for a standard placing of stamps. Otherwise it would be almost impossible to have the worldwide service that we all take for granted.
M. Magowan
Sunderland.

FACT!

In 1909 the US Federal Government impounded 40 barrels of Coca Cola and charged the company with violation of the Pure Food Act because the coca ingredient implied the presence of the illegal drug cocaine.

Why are three brass balls used as a sign by pawnbrokers?

The three brass balls (or, to be correct, golden balls) used as a sign by pawnbrokers were adopted from the arms of the Medici family of Florence, who between the 15th and 18th centuries were leading bankers and financiers. The balls are mostly wooden and gilded over.

My family were pawnbrokers and in the mid-1930's my uncle replaced his sign with three golden coloured glass orbs each fitted with an electric bulb. He claimed to be the only man in Nottingham whose balls lit up at night.
Leonard Gaskin
Mapperley, Nottingham.

The three brass balls outside a pawnbroker's shop are to indicate that the odds are 2 to 1 against you getting some money back!
Mr H.G. Huyton
St Helens, Lancs.

St. Nicholas is the patron saint of pawnbrokers! Tradition has it that he tossed three gold balls, or three bags of gold, through a window, each landed in a girl's stocking and saved them from being sold into prostitution!
Revd. Canon B.R. Pearson
Harrogate, North Yorks.

Well you've heard of giving a pound of flesh - the brass balls are to remind you that it's always going to cost you more than you're prepared to give and definitely more than you've got!
Catherine Swanson
Inkberrow, Worcestershire.

The three brass balls (or golden balls) outside a pawnbrokers are meant to represent three gold coins. A gold coin is called a 'bezant' so this is why the three balls are so named.
Laura Bezant (age 12)
Maidstone, Kent.

Why do we put a cross on a ballot paper, rather than a tick?

Prior to 1872 people recorded their vote by word of mouth. As some people were afraid to announce their particular allegiance the secret ballot was introduced. In view of the large number of illiterates, the cross, an already accepted form of 'making one's mark', was considered the easier option.
Colin Blomeley
Liskeard, Cornwall.

The cross is a traditional and uncomplicated 'signature' and dates back to the times when such a symbol was sufficient as the 'mark' for those who were illiterate. Legally, I understand, a cross still satisfies the demand for an autograph, and the suitability of it on a ballot paper is further enhanced by its universal interpretation as a sign of adamant declaration.
Richard Kay
Pulborough, West Sussex.

A cross needs to be made deliberately by drawing one line, lifting the pen from the paper and crossing the first line. If a tick were used, then a simple slip of the pen could end up looking like a positive endorsement of perhaps an unwanted candidate.
Lorna McKie
Glasgow.

To place an X on a ballot paper rather than a tick is an admission that whoever you vote for will be sure to get it wrong!
N. Dickens
Manchester.

A cross on ballot papers symbolises drawn daggers, indicating that the fight is on. Opposing sides are preparing to cut one another's throats. Verbally of course.
Colin E. Clarke
Matlock, Derbyshire.

Why 'Mayday' and 'SOS' instead of a simple 'help'?

Mayday is the international distress call by radiotelephony (speech) and is the phonetic equivalent in English of the French phrase *m'aidez*, meaning 'help me'.

The first distress call by wireless telegraphy (morse code) was CQD and was introduced by the Marconi Company on 1 February 1904, and was derived from CQ, the general call to 'all ships', with the addition of D for distress.

CQD, however, is a massive jumble of dots and dashes in morse code, easily lost or misheard in atmospherics. The international Radio Telegraphic Convention held in Berlin in 1906 was given the task of finding something better and came us with SOS. These are not the initial letters of anything but were simply chosen as the written representation of a sound in morse code - the letters VTB or many other combinations of letters produce the same sound of three dots, three dashes, three dots.

SOS won immediate approval as the international distress call by wireless telegraphy because when transmitted correctly it has a compelling rhythm in morse code which commands immediate attention - d'd'd'dah dah dah d'd'dit.
C.H. Milsom
Upton, Wirral.

It is said that the Titanic was the first ship to send an SOS which led to speculation as to whether or not some ships that could have offered quicker assistance actually realised that the distress signal had changed from CQD to SOS.
R.A. Smith
Bournemouth, Dorset.

'Mayday' was universally adopted as a distress signal because it is easy to remember, instantly recognisable, and presents no pronunciation problems to speakers in any language. I worked mainly in morse code during my 27 year career in the Navy, and the ominous sound of the morse distress distress signal 'SOS' is also chillingly recognisable among the bewildering uproar of other signals on congested morse wavelengths. On hearing it all other operators immediately ceased their own transmissions in order to allow the vital details of the disaster to be communicated without any airwave interference. I've heard it a few times myself, and can vouch for the fact that a sombre 'SOS' can silence all other traffic in seconds. . .
Bernard Campion
Plymouth, Devon.

Mayday is the anglicisation of *m'aidez*, which means help me. For some reason safety signals are drawn from the French even though English is the lingua franca of maritime communications. There are others; Pan, from Panne or mishap, which is one down from mayday; Securite, which again is one level less urgent; Silence, and Silence Finis.
Alan Gordon
Shoreham by Sea,
West Sussex.

CASPARED?

How does the person who drives the snow plough get to work in the morning?

FACT!

The first aeroplane fitted with a lavotary was the Russian passenger transport Russky Vitiaz in 1913.

CASPARED?

How does the non-stick coating stick to the pan in the first place?

Why does the tax year end at the start of April?

The tax year ends in April since Aries is the most propitious zodiac sign for requesting details of income and outgoings. When Aries is in the ascendant, individuals involved in finance exhibit great willpower, are obstinate and resent all criticism. The overlapping of the cusp during the first week of April allows the massing of great fortunes.

It should also be noted that the birthstone for the cusp of the tax year is the bloodstone.

Noel Turnbull
Newcastle upon Tyne.

The main reason taxes are not collected at the end of every calendar year is due to the fact that the Government realise that after Christmas shopping nobody would have any money left.

C. Green
Manchester.

The tax year always used to coincide with the old year, which began on 25 March instead of 1 January. In 1752 11 days were lost to bring us into line with the Gregorian calendar, as used by other European countries. Hence the beginning of the year was in effect moved from 25 March to 5 April. Although the calender year now starts on 1 January, the tax year has kept the 18th century tradition.

James Luckhurst,
Hampton, Middlesex.

We are all aware of the saying 'A fool and his money are soon parted' and our national celebration of the day known as All Fools. The government have simply used this information to their advantage when collecting taxes.

E. Gryks
Romford, Essex.

Why is a 99 ice cream called a 99?

A 99 ice cream is called a 99 as the flake is exactly 99mm in length.

The flake is specifically made for the ice cream trade. You will notice the difference in size and shape (it being more sturdy) than the traditional flake (being crumbly) you purchase in the shops.

Due to its size the name became popular and is now used by all to describe an ice cream with a flake in it.
Michael Geoghegan
Boothstown, Manchester.

There is a town in Lancashire called Nelson and on Railway Street of that town there used to be, before the war, a sweets and ice cream shop. The number of the shop was 99 Railway Street, the person who owned the shop was a Mr Catley and at that time he sold very good ice cream. His speciality was an ice cream cornet with a Cadburys chocolate flake pushed in to the ice cream cornet. This delightful confection was very popular and eventually became known as a '99'. As there was a cinema just across from Mr Catley's shop, a slide would be put on the screen advertising his now famous '99 ice cream'. Mr Catley continued to sell this until the wartime shortages curtailed his sales, when sweet rationing forced him to close his shop.
Kenneth Clarke
Nelson, Lancashire.

It's short for **IC**e Cream. (it must have been invented in Roman times).
William McCrea
Preston, Lancashire.

'Ice Cream 99', originated in 1929 and was the number on the door of Dunkley's ice cream parlour, 99 Wellington Street, Gorton, Manchester, unfortunately now demolished.
Mr J. Fitton
Highcliffe on Sea, Dorset.

How can one determine the four corners of the globe?

Everyone knows we are all on a flat, square earth. If you could draw diagonals, they would meet at Nelson's Column, which is of course the centre of the world. The term globe is merely an advertising gimmick!
George Crosby
Weston super Mare.

Obviously, today, the expression cannot be interpreted literally. It is used, rather more poetically, to mean simply 'the whole world over' or 'everywhere in the world'. The French have the same idiomatic expression - *'les quatre coins du monde'*.

The idea probably dates back to the time when the world was generally thought to be flat. The four corners were then the most remote parts or regions of the world, as it was known to the person using the term. It is interesting to note that the idea of 'four' also exists in the expression 'in all quarters', meaning everywhere in general. No doubt, this refers to the four cardinal points north, south, east and west.

Today, with lots of people travelling all over the world, as well as round the world, the saying has lost its literal meaning.
Noel Blackham
Edgbaston, Birmingham.

The four corners of the globe comes from a quote from the Bible: Revelations 7, v. 1 - 'After this I saw four Angels standing at the four corners of the earth. . .'

It refers to the four compass points of North, South, East, and West (not right angled corners at all) at which four of God's Angels are posted to control the power of the winds.
Sheila Parnaby
Haxby, North Yorkshire.

'Corners', is a convenient way of referring to areas of the earth (individually covering several thousand square miles) where the gravitational pull is measurably greatest. These were named in 1965 by members of the Johns Hopkins Applied Physics Laboratory as being located in Ireland, south east of the Cape of Good Hope, west of the Peruvian coast, and between New Guinea and Japan. Each of these areas is some 120ft above the geodetic mean. In general terms, the phrase has always been used to refer to the remotest parts of the world.

John Deamer
Broadstairs, Kent.

Rather than our corners of the globe Shakespeare claims three in King John:

Come the three corners of
  the world in arms,
And we shall shock them,
Nought shall us rue,
If England to itself do rest
  but true.

Siobhan O'Brian
Hale Barns, Cheshire.

Although the earth is a globe and therefore cannot have actual corners, the expression 'four corners of the globe' is in actual fact a mathematical one.

What you do is to draw a circle round the earth starting at the north pole, through the south pole and back to the north pole. You then draw a similar line at exactly ninety degrees to the first, through the north and south poles. Each of these lines will then cross the equator at two equidistant points. These points are thus the four corners of the world.

Mike Harrison
Warminster, Wiltshire.

FACT!

A 'Valium Picnic' is the term for a slow day on the New York Stock Exchange.

FACT!

Michael Jackson and Lenny Henry were both born on 29 August 1958.

What is the origin of the two-fingered gesture of contempt?

Just before the Battle of Agincourt in 1415 the French soldiers, confident of victory, threatened that once they had won the battle they would cut off the index and middle fingers of every longbowman so that they would never be able to use their weapons again. On hearing this threat the English began using the two fingered salute to the enemy as gesture of defiance which has carried on to this day.
Celeste Hicks
Darlington, County Durham.

The reason goes back to the Dark Ages when the inverted 'V' was said to ward off the Devil by blocking his horns. Thus to flash the V-sign at someone was to wish ill fortune upon them.
Rodney James
Branston, Staffordshire.

Winston Churchill was seldom without a large cigar. To acknowledge cheers he would remove the cigar from his mouth and wave. The most comfortable way to carry a cigar is between the first two fingers thus forming a 'V'. The gesture caught on and the rest is history.
It is generally considered 'V for Victory' if you show the palm and a mortal insult if you display the back of your hand. This distinction is seldom appreciated in the USA. Many Americans admire Churchill and sometimes make what to them is a pro-British gesture only to have their motives misunderstood in a most distressing way. Churchill, with his American mother and his thorough knowledge of history, should have known better.
D. S. Adamson
Gillingham, Kent.

Do, or did, prisoners ever wear uniforms with arrows on them?

In 1919 at the age of ten years in the Isle of Wight, I clearly remember seeing convicts at work in the vicinity of Parkhurst prison. They were all wearing greyish-yellow jackets and trousers on which were stamped large black arrows. I was told at the time that the convicts wore boots whose soles were studded with nails in arrow pattern to assist tracking should they escape.
G. Ashdown
Bournemouth, Dorset.

I would have thought arrows were the most appropriate thing in a place called Dartmoor.
K. Clegg
Oldham, Lancashire.

By 1849, the Australians had become extremely reluctant to accept any more convicts from Britain and the need for prisons in this country became apparent. Pentonville prison was built and at the same time it was decided that prisoners should be identified by the wearing of a uniform displaying a broad arrow. This system was retained until Alexander Paterson's reforms of 1921.
Richard Stanton
HM Prison Service
High Down, Surrey.

In the Royal Navy men under punishment and sentenced to cells for 90 days did. A white calico two piece uniform with broad arrows, up to and including the Second World War.
E. R. Saunders
Paignton, South Devon.

The broad arrow is the symbol used to indicate government property. I think it is still used to this day and was at one time even stamped on pencils in government offices.
Albert Simister
Bispham, Blackpool.

Why do we eat hot cross buns at Easter?

Although this is today a Christian custom, it is certainly not a Christian invention.

Hot cross buns first occurred in Chaldean (moonworship) rites. The buns were used in the worship of the Goddess Eostre (Easter) during a springtime sacrificial festival named after her. Her sacred month was 'Eastre monath', the Moon of Easter.

These sacred cakes, composed chiefly of flour and honey, were offered up to the Goddess. The cross symbolised the four quarters of the moon.
Elizabeth Bilas
Cheltenham,
Gloucestershire.

Because they are 50 times healthier than chocolate Easter eggs.
Mrs G. Bowditch
Solihull, West Midlands.

The ingredients of the bun are seen as symbolic.
Flour reminds us of the bread at the Last Supper.
Dried fruits remind us of the vine and the wine drunk at the Last Supper.
Spices remind us of the spices used to prepare Jesus' body for the burial.
Yeast reminds us of how Jesus rose from the dead.
The cross on the bun reminds us of the crucifixion on the first Good Friday.
Matthew Redman (Aged 11)
Blaenavon, Gwent.

FACT!

In 1988, Luciano Pavarotti received 165 curtain calls and the applause continued for over an hour after appearing in *L'elisir d'amore* at the Deutsche Opera in Berlin.

In mediaeval times, bakers marked all their loaves with a cross to ward off evil spirits and encourage the dough to rise. The crosses were only later taken to represent the crucifixion.
Mrs S. Watson
Carnoustie, Angus.

Traditional folklore has it that hot cross buns are descended from the pagan days when the vernal equinox was celebrated. If properly made on the same day, Good Friday, they are supposed to protect the whole family from fires, rats, accidents and shipwrecks. A cheap form of insurance, in fact!
Mrs K. Peters-Gauld,
Northampton.

This tradition stems back to 1361, when at St Albans Abbey buns were given to the local poor. The buns were made from the dough left over after making the sacramental bread on Good Friday. By the 18th century hot cross buns were very popular and were usually eaten at breakfast, warm from the oven.
This aside, the origins of a bun bearing a cross date back to the Greeks and Romans, who both ate small wheaten cakes marked with a cross to celebrate their pagan spring festivals.
Derek Mellor,
Cheltenham,
Gloucestershire.

FACT!

The highest number of equal folds that can be put into a piece of square paper can never be more than ten - regardless of the size of paper.

CASPARED?

Where do ice cream vans go during the winter?

FACT!

The UK drinks more tea than all the other EC countries put together.

Who first used a soapbox for a political speech, and where?

The use of a political soapbox must surely have come about thousands of years ago when any leader or potential leader wished to speak to the masses. It would obviously not have been a soapbox that was first used, but instead something that would have raised the speaker above the heads of the crowd. Perhaps a table of some kind, a cart or something similar was used.
Sarah Hutton
Little Lever, Bolton.

Governor Coke Stevenson of Texas was the first politician to use a soapbox, in the 1940's. His campaigning style was to go out and talk to the people. In fact, in our own recent election campaigns, John Major was very much a Coke Stevenson, to Neil Kinnock's Lyndon Johnson.
Sandra Berman
Chandlers Ford, Hants.

The first recorded use of a soapbox was said to have been in 1820. However, the first evidence I have of an actual speaker is of a Mr A. Prentice, who spoke for the anti-Corn Law League on Thursday, 12 August 1853.
Mrs E. Palmer
Porthcawl, Mid Glamorgan.

It was obviously an orator who wanted to make sure his speech wasn't a wash-out.
Chris Hand
Chichester, West Sussex.

It was probably by a very short politician who wished to air his dirty linen outside a laundrette.
R. Radnell
Halton, Leeds.

I've no idea, but if it is of any help I can guess what he held shares in.
Steve Hall
Mildenhall, Suffolk.

Where do jokes come from?

Jokes my friend come from everyday life and literally any ordinary situation. All that happens is that somebody sees the joke and passes on the observation for other people to share.
Bernard Manning
Comedian
Manchester.

Jokes come from adversity in the layman and hunger from the gag writer.
Diana Piercy
West Clandon, Surrey.

A joke is just a group of words that appear funny to certain people. If you don't believe me try telling the one you heard in the pub last night to the ladies' chorus of your local amateur Operatic Society!
John Maguire
Stockport, Cheshire.

FACT!

The Beach Boys formed their band in 1961, and although their first single was called *Surfin '*, only one of the band could actually surf.

FACT!

Dustin Hoffman, the American filmstar, worked as a psychiatric attendant and a children's toy demonstrator before hitting the big time.

FACT!

One of the top ten causes of stress related illness is reconciliation with a wife or husband after a separation or argument.

Is it true that the kilt was invented by an Englishman?

The first type of kilt was made in Scotland in the 16th century. It was originally an all in one item cut above the knee and belted in the middle. In the 18th Century it was made into a two-piece item of clothing, consisting of a little kilt and the plaid, the plaid being a woollen tartan cloak.
Christopher McCaul
Co. Donegal, Ireland.

Tartan design originates from Holland and kilts from England. In 1727 a Lancashire weaver invented a new style of clothing: the kilt, designed for working men and based on the old Saxon smock. At the same time, but completely separately, tartan designs were imported into England from Holland. Tartans eventually became part of uniforms which differentiated new regiments of the army.

Then two brothers claiming to be descended from the Royal Stuart family produced a document which purported to show that mediaeval clans each had their own tartan pattern. In 1844 the brothers published a book which allowed all Scots people to find their clan tartan from their surname. Now Scots all over the world have celebrated their Scottishness in the tartan kilts.
Lorna Davis
Reading.

The kilt was invented by an Englishman and a Scotsman. They were called C. ROSS-DRESSER AND T.V. CALEDONIAN.
Tim Hopkins
Luton.

The kilt was invented by the Romans and worn by all ranks in the Roman Legions: from the Legate or General of a Legion to the lowliest legionnaire. Naturally the higher the rank the better the quality and design. As to how the Picts, as they were better known at that time, came to adopt the kilt is a mystery but it could have been taken from the IV Legion, which supposedly disappeared on an expedition into Scotland.

K. V. Semmens
Sudbury, Suffolk.

A few years ago my husband and I visited Egypt and while being taken round a museum by an Egyptian guide our attention was drawn to a huge statue of one of the Pharaohs and she said 'Notice his skirt, which we call a - yes - a "KILT"'!!! So I fear that the kilt was around a long time before it ended up on the British scene.

Mrs Lydia Littman
Israel.

FACT!

Over £15 million is spent each year in Great Britain on the purchase of laxatives.

CASPARED?

The rubber used for car tyres can last for tens of thousands of miles before wearing out, so why isn't it used for the soles of shoes which wear out after only a few hundred miles?

CASPARED?

Why can we always remember when we wake up, but never remember when we fall asleep?

CASPARED?

If there is enough food to go round, why does everyone get a square meal?

Why do we put candles on a birthday cake?

The customs of offering congratulations, presenting gifts, and celebrating the birthday with lighted candles were meant to protect the birthday celebrant from evil spirits and demons and to ensure security for the coming year. Down to the 4th century AD Christianity rejected birthday celebrations as pagan customs.

The custom of using lighted candles began with the Greeks. Honey cakes in the shape of the moon and lit with tapers were placed on the temple altar of Artemis. Candles are used because they are supposedly endowed with special magic for granting wishes.
Kevin Price
Preston, Lancs.

Candles are used to hide the mistakes we made whilst icing the cake.
Susan James
Pontefract, West Yorkshire.

Astrologers consider the sun's position at birth to indicate the strength of a person's heart and therefore the measure of vital energy available to survive in physical form. It is our battery power on which we run and is recharged annually when the sun reaches the same birth position, hence we wish people Many Happy (Solar) Returns.

Just before our birthday we flag, energy runs low and so the candle flames are a symbolic reassurance that the spirit of life in us is about to be renewed. The older we get the more candle power we need to give us new hope for the year ahead, until finally like the candle, we snuff it!
Ron Gwynn
Fleet, Hants.

We use candles because lightbulbs would look silly.
Nick Setchfield
Cyncoed, Cardiff.

Why is yellow the colour of cowardice?

The reason that the colour yellow is associated with cowardice goes back to the middle ages.

Sufferers of jaundice, in an age when medical afflictions were believed to indicate weaknesses of character, were supposed to be receiving punishment for sins of cowardice, jealousy, and betrayal.

The association with the colour yellow as a symbol of cowardice is therefore a logical progression of this belief.
Nick Sessions
Ashbourne, Derbyshire.

In France the doors of traitors used to be daubed with yellow.
Robert Millar
Ballyclare, Co. Antrim.

FACT!

The most popular name for a dog in the UK is Sam.

The reason for this is that when feelings of cowardice are experienced by individuals there is often a simultaneous desire to urinate, the colour of which has, over the years, been simplified to resemble the colour yellow.
Alan Aziz
London NW4.

Down through the ages some people, such as clairvoyants have claimed to see an aura of colours surrounding the human form. Different qualities of character are attributed to the different colours. Dull, muddy or weak yellows have been associated with negative traits including timidity, selfishness, and weakness of will. Positively, the pure yellows are associated with spiritual and creative love, logic, and wisdom.
Miss N. Smith
Lelant, Cornwall.

I always believed that the colour of cowardice was white, as in the three white feathers type, but thanks for the information. The next war that comes along, I'll make sure I look out for my three yellow feathers as well.
John Cross
Camden Town, London.

Chickens, when young, are coloured yellow and are naturally timid and easily frightened.

We associate this fear with the animals' colour, hence the taunt 'chicken', when somebody is afraid to do something.
Miss A.J. Randall
Great Barr, Birmingham.

Yellow is the colour of cowardice and stems from the rhyme 'Cowardy, Cowardy, Custard'. Well, custard is yellow isn't it?
Helen Collins
Great Wyrley, Staffs.

CASPARED?

Why is a second opinion more valid than the first?

FACT!

The Bolzano Region of Italy has more native German speakers than native Italian speakers.

CASPARED?

Does a zebra have a black body with white stripes, or a white body with black stripes?

CASPARED?

Why do promotion packs run out at supermarkets just when you need two more tokens?

CASPARED?

How do dockleaves know how to grow next to nettles?

Who invented swearing?

The first man to hit his thumb with a hammer.
Janice Loveday
St Peter, Buckinghamshire.

Swearing was originally used only by way of taking an oath in God's name. Later it was extended to bad language by the use of these sacred expressions as expletives. The Greek philosopher Pythagoras cursed by the number four and Ionians swore by the cabbage. The French poet Baudelaire swore by the 'sacred onion' and a friend of mine always exploded with 'by the holy cheese and rice'. In 1745, labourers could be fined one shilling per oath. If a gentleman swore, every oath uttered cost him five shillings. Women were considerably more fortunate, they could swear for nothing!
It is still illegal to swear in the Royal Parks.
Rhoda Watson
Newtownabbey, Co Antrim.

No one invented swearing. Taboo words have been around since oral communication began. In the English-speaking world, the most severe words are associated with sex, closely followed by excretion and the Christian religion. Such words are seen as offensive because of traditionally placed emphasis on sexual morality in our culture.
Neil Huntingdon
Goole, North Humberside.

Swearing was not invented by a swearer, but by a listener. The first person to be shocked by what someone else had said invented swearing. Descendants of this person keep swearing alive today, by unwittingly endowing swearing with a potency it doesn't deserve.
Without people who notice, swearing would very quickly become redundant.
Tim Hopkins
Luton, Beds.

CHAPTER

SIX

THIS SPORTING LIFE

Who invented the first ball game?

The first ball game was called 'pok-ta-pok', an ancient version of our modern basketball. The Olmecs first played this around the 10th century BC. It was similar to other games played around that time in that it was a form of fertility rite performed at religious festivals.
Richard Brogan
Strabane, County Tyrone.

Hockey as we would recognise the game was played around 510 BC in Greece. However, a wall relief in an Egyptian tomb depicts two players in the bully position and has been dated to about 2000 BC.
  Polo, then known as Pula, was played in Persia in the 5th century BC and a form of football, Tsu-Chin, was popular in China during the 3rd and 4th centuries BC.
Colin Blomeley
Liskeard, Cornwall.

Eve, when she threw the apple at Adam and shouted 'Catch'!
Steve Szubert
Ulverston, Cumbria.

The first ball games go as far back as 3100 BC. They were invented by the Egyptians and were played by Egyptian children. The balls were made out of leather and were stuffed with grain. Many Egyptian tomb paintings show these games being played but unfortunately nobody knows the rules of how they were played.
Miss L Illinesi
Woking, Surrey.

By the way he goes on with himself about one particular ball game, I am in no doubt that it must have been Jimmy Hill!
Morag McGlennon
Dundee.

What is the origin of the term 'love' in tennis?

I would suggest that it is derived from the French *'l'oeuf'*: the shape of the egg which corresponds to the digit for nought or zero. The 'egg' concept is also found in the cricket term for nought or no score, i.e. 'duck' which is a contraction for 'duck-egg' when applied to a scoreless innings in cricket.
M.A. Nield
Blackburn, Lancs.

Love, representing nil is a corruption of the French word for egg as this is the approximate shape of a handwritten zero.
Many tennis terms are derived from the French language, and stem from a clock being used as a scoring instrument.

To indicate the scoring of a point one hand would be moved through a quarter hour, thus the first point would be 15, the second 30, and the third 40 (the five having been dropped from common usage).

If at forty both players achieved the same score both hands of the clock would be put at twelve o'clock or the *'douze'* position, *douze* eventually becoming deuce.
Stewart Ramsbottom
Peel Green, Manchester.

I agree with most of your readers about tennis terms but Stewart Ramsbottom has got it totally wrong about 'deuce'.

This is not a corruption of *douze* at all. What has twelve o'clock got to do with deuce in tennis?

The real origin is in the word *'deux'*, meaning best of two points to play. The same usage is found amongst card players who say Ace, Deuce, Tray, for one, two, three - in the same way.
Norman Allen
Hemel Hempstead, Herts.

Why are there 18 holes on a golf course?

In Scotland, where the modern game originally evolved, golf was played on common ground and took place among many other activities, the number of holes depending on the amount of ground available. At St. Andrews, play was to a number of holes leading north-westward from the town, then homeward to the same holes. At one time it was the custom to play 22 holes but this became 18 in 1764 and, given the pre-eminence of St. Andrews, 18 became the number of holes for a normal golf course everywhere.

Keith Wright
English Golf Union
Leicester.

If there had only been 17 it would have had him home in time to bathe the kids and if there were 19 it wouldn't have left him time for a quick one in the bar.

Diana Piercy
West Clandon, Surrey.

Most people know that golf was invented in St. Andrews by a shepherd who used to hit grass divots with his inverted crook, as a diversion from playing his bagpipes. His day was divided into three, three-hourly shifts stretching from dawn until dusk. In between he ate haggis and neeps and invented other games like tossing the caber and shinty, and kept himself warm by dancing the Highland Fling and drinking whisky. The shepherd timed his working journey from meadow to meadow per every half hour, so during the long summer daylight hours from start to finish he successfully covered 18 meadows, marking each with a stick with a little flag on it just in case anyone was looking for him. His 19th port of call was the pub which was called the 19th watering hole. . .

J. E. Corrigan
Buxton, Derbyshire.

Who was the first person to test a parachute?

The use of the parachute coincided with the development of the hot-air balloon in the late 18th century.

On 22 October 1797, Andre Jacques Garnerin ascended from the Parc de Nonceau, Paris in a parachute of his own design hung beneath a balloon. When he reached about 3000 feet he pulled out the cords holding it to the balloon, and came down safely.

Garnerin also made the first parachute descent in England on 21 September 1802, from a balloon which was sent up from Grosvenor Square, London. The first person to descend from an aircraft in flight was Albert Berry, an American, on 1 March 1912, over St. Louis, Missouri.

The modern ripcord folded parachute strapped to the flier was first used by Leslie Leroy Irvin, who jumped on 19 April 1919 over McCook Field, Dayton, Ohio.
Fred Lake
Walton on Thames, Surrey.

The first parachute drop in England was in June 1785, when Jean-Pierre Blanchard, using a chute designed by himself, and using a pet 'moggie' as the parachutist, dropped this unlikely load from the basket of his balloon. He demonstrated this drop several times during the month over open ground in London. Blanchard, perhaps one of the first professional aeronauts of the age, claimed that he had himself made two drops using 'chutes' of his design, in France, during 1777 and again in 1783.

It may be of interest to note that Leonardo da Vinci made some sketches of what could have been a successful parachute in 1498.
Douglas Dix
Kirkbymoorside, N. Yorks.

Who invented the pole vault and why?

The exact origins of pole vaulting are unknown but is almost certain that it is a descendant of pole jumping, a means of obtaining distance rather than height using a long pole.

It is known that pole jumping was popular in the 16th Century and that Henry VII was an exponent. However, it is believed that a form of pole jumping took place in Ireland at the Tailtean Games long before the start of the Ancient Greek Olympics. But it was not until the mid-19th century that it became a competitive sport in a form similar to modern day pole vaulting.

The Lake District was a stronghold, and the first record of a contest was at Penrith in 1843. By then the object was to lever oneself over a bar and the English style of vaulting, devised in Ulverston, entailed climbing up the pole and then travelling over the bar in a sitting position.

There was another style which was based on the modern day vaulting style which banned 'climbing'. It was this form that became the standard for pole vault competitions and the event was included in the Amateur Club Championships of 1866. Perhaps surprisingly, climbing was not totally banned by the AAA until 1919.

Ian Morrison
Runcorn, Cheshire.

The pole vault was invented in the the old East Germany by people who wanted to be in West Germany.

Brian Hargreaves
Elland, West Yorkshire.

The pole vault started as pole jumping in the Fen District of eastern England to leap over marshy ground. Competitive jumping started in the mid-1800's at Ulverston in Lancashire.

Michael Jakeman
Birmingham.

What is the purpose of the little indentations on golf balls?

In the mid 19th century golf ball makers were looking for a replacement for the featherie golf ball (a leather, feather filled ball). They experimented with gutta-percha, a gum produced by Malayan trees. The original 'gutties' were completely smooth, resulting in the ball flying erratically and ducking to earth after travelling only a short distance. It soon became apparent that the ball flew much better after some use and that cuts and bruises actually improved its efficiency, therefore the making of artificial indentations was developed. To this day manufacturers still experiment with the size, shape, number and pattern of these 'dimples' in order to produce a ball which flies further and straighter.

Chris Thompson
Droitwich, Worcs.

The solution is simply one of aerodynamics. Hold for example a teaspoon by the tip of its handle so that the bowl can have a reasonable degree of swing, then hold it under the down draught from the blower of an electric hand drier. You soon get the idea. The teaspoon swings, drawn into the down draught by the forces exerted on the bowl. This is the principle which keeps a golf ball flying so to speak, once it has been hit. The combined volition and spin create a streamlined boundary layer of air over the pitted surface, for added lift.

Jennifer O. French
London.

They are there for filling with mud, thus providing a market for the makers of novelty golf ball cleaners.

Miss Helen Bailey
Northwich, Cheshire.

Why are local football games called 'Derby Matches'?

Since the 14th century a game of 'mob football' has been played every Shrove Tuesday in Ashbourne, Derbyshire, between people from the north of the town (the uptowners), and those from the south (the downtowners) with the divide being determined by Henmore Brook, a stream running through the centre of the town. In time this became known as the Derby game. As the game spread, other matches between local teams also eventually became known as Derby matches or local Derbies.
Barry McIntosh
Bexleyheath, Kent.

Probably because most of the haircuts sported by the players would look better on a horse!
Miss Shan Frost
Warfield, Berkshire.

In the 18th century there grew up the fierce Shrove Tuesday games, the most famous taking place in Derby when the young men of the parish of All Saints challenged those of the parish of St. Peter. All men over the age of eighteen took part, trying to force the ball from one parish into another, each parish representing the goal.

In 1731 the Mayor of that year made an unsuccessful attempt to suppress the game. This happened every year until 1848 when the Mayor read the Riot Act and troops were called in. So ended the Derby game. From then on a 'local derby' was attributed to a football match played with a fierce partisanship between neighbouring clubs.
Mel Hopkins
Kettering, Northants.

Why do we use the term 'hat trick' in football?

The term 'hat trick' was actually first used in the game of cricket. When a bowler took three wickets with three successive balls he was entitled to a new hat at the expense of the club. It should be worth noting that this was not the origination of the term 'bowler hat', that came from a corruption of its designer's name, Beaulieu.

Clive Whichelow
London SW19.

It's really a cricket term and dates from the times when first class cricket was generally played by gentlemen rather than the working classes, with players often taking to the field wearing a hat.

Until outlawed later, players often used to catch the ball in the hat rather than in the hands. The term trick is common in older English for three (still used in card games). Hence three catches became known as a hat trick. The term has since evolved to mean any three scores or successes in sport of all kinds.

M. Carnell
Whitestone, Warwickshire.

CASPARED?

Why is Jessica Fletcher always in the vicinity when a murder is committed?

CASPARED?

What were barn owls called before the advent of the barn?

FACT!

In 1945, starlings resting on Big Ben slowed the minute hand by five minutes.

The term originated from one Colonel Peter Hawker, a noted 18th century sportsman and shot, who, when sport was slow, would toss his hat in the air and invite his companions to shoot at it. To anyone who managed to hit the hat three times in succession (no mean feat with black powder and a muzzle-loading gun) he would present a bottle of his home-made sloe gin, one brand of which still carries his name to this day.
John Parkman
Tunbridge Wells, Kent.

The origin of the term is to be found in the history of Canadian ice hockey. When a player scored three goals in one game it became traditional for spectators to throw their hats into the air as a form of accolade.

Over time, achieving three things in many aspects of life became known as a 'hat trick', especially when scoring even one is considered difficult.
M. Girouard
Tadworth, Surrey.

FACT!

The first sporting event to be filmed was the Oxford and Cambridge Boat Race of 1895.

FACT!

The Earth's glaciers and ice caps contain as much water as has flowed in all the Earth's rivers in the past 1000 years.

CASPARED?

Why does the person in front of you at the supermarket queue always have more interesting food than you do?

CASPARED?

If girlie magazines are supposed to give you bad eyesight, why are they always displayed on the top shelf, where no one can see them?

Why are numbers on a dartboard in such a strange order?

There is no complicated answer to this question. The numbering on a dartboard is as ingenious as it is irritating.

The sequence is designed to prevent easy scoring and encourage accuracy by the placement of low numbers either side of the high ones: 20 (5 and 1), 19 (3 and 7), 18 (1 and 4). The left hand side of the dartboard is the best to throw at if you are new to the game, as it features fairly high numbers: 12, 9, 14, 11, 8, and 16. Provided that all three darts hit their targets, you are assured of an average score. This side of the board is known as 'the married man's side' meaning always playing it safe.

Who actually devised the numbering system in the first place is still unknown, and today remains a mystery.

Patrick Chaplin
Maldon, Essex.

It really doesn't matter where the numbers are, I can never hit the dartboard anyway.

Jim Bowen
Bullseye.

If the person who invented the dartboard consumed as much alcohol as the average player, the reason the numbers are in such a strange order becomes apparent.

Matthew Hedgecote
Barnet, Herts.

If you have ever tried writing the numbers one to twenty around the outside of a circle, or even devising a simple pattern to put them in, you will notice that it produces a strange one-sided effect.

The board looks much better now, with random numbers and is also easier to aim at.

Miss L Stewart.
Abingdon, Oxon.

CHAPTER
SEVEN

NATURE WATCH

What do you call a male ladybird?

Reference to any good encyclopaedia will reveal that ladybirds belong to the family coccinellidae. It therefore follows that the male members of this family are called either Mr Coccinellidae or Master Coccinellidae, depending upon their age. Of course, in practice, such formal address would only be used on equally formal occasions, for instance, during introductions at the annual Moth Ball or when applying to appear in television advertisements for beer. Research has shown that in private circles most ladybirds, male and female, are affectionately known as spot.
T.P. Kemish
Southampton.

In the U.S.A., back in the 1960's, Ladybird's husband was called LBJ!
(Lyndon Barnes Johnson).
Ian Lawes
Brighton.

I always call mine a Transvest-mite!
S.V. Lukins
Street, Somerset.

The term 'ladybird' was coined after Our Lady, presumably to flatter. It is a neutral term and hence contains no hint as to the sex of the insect, so we are obliged to refer to a male ladybird as just that. Not for long, perhaps? So as not to cause any embarrassment to ladybirds, particularly male ladybirds, maybe we ought to follow the example of certain anti-sexist activities. Perhaps then these little creatures can be more fairly described as 'personbirds', or would this be taking anti-sexism to a ridiculous and confusing extreme.
Ceri Williams
Great Dunmow, Essex.

You call him spotted dick, and I'm not saying why.
Emma Taylor
Leicester.

May I suggest Paul? After all, this colourful individual has developed from a spotty beatle into a character of note, who uses wings to his advantage.

Generally recognised as a good friend of our environment, it could also be said that his intolerance of pests has become something of a consuming passion.
Derrick Francis
Daventry, Northants.

Most definitely a laddybird!
Ms W. Shepherd
Manningtree, Essex.

After extensive research into this question, I can conclusively claim that you can call a male ladybird anything you like, and it won't take offence.
A. Lewis
Ilford, Essex.

I would call him highly promiscuous as he normally mates with an average of 20 partners in late spring at up to seven hours at a time.
Mrs R. Evans
Linden Village, Bucks.

137

What colour were dinosaurs?

Fossils and bones tell us much about what dinosaurs looked like, but nothing is known about skin colour. In an article in the *Boston Globe*, Charles Schaff, collection manager in charge of fossil vertebrates at Harvard's Museum of Comparative Zoology, says that no one has any scientific proof about the colour. The browns and greens of some museum specimens are the artists' impression of what the colour might have been, but Schaff thinks they could have been more highly coloured as are the males of many species in order to attract a mate.
Mrs Geraldine Rogers, Guildford.

Since it is impossible to tell what colour dinosaurs were from their skeletons, experts can only guess. For example, herbivores would probably have been a greenish brown to blend in with surrounding vegetation. Carnivores may have been the same colour as the herbivores so that they could attack them unexpectedly, or brighter colours to act as a warning for any possible victims. Ocean-bound dinosaurs (like the plesiosaurus) could have been blue for the same reason.
Tim McCarthy, Bagshot, Surrey.

CASPARED?

How do pebbles know how to get into a shoe, but never know how to get out?

There is no evidence during that period when dinosaurs flourished any living organism had the ability to recognise colours as we do. Consequently, dinosaurs were, to all intents and purposes, colourless.
D. Thorp, Manchester.

Why don't sleeping birds fall off their perches?

My pet parrot tells me birds don't actually sleep, they just meditate a lot.
John Sherriff
Exhall, West Midlands.

Like its bill, a bird's foot has adapted to fit in with its way of life which depends on the habitats where it lives, feeds, breeds, and of course sleeps. Perching birds include the vast majority of small birds, and they have a special tendon at the back of the leg which, very cleverly, tightens the toes as the leg is bent, so automatically keeping the bird on its perch as it sleeps. Each species of bird has the design of foot best suited to its lifestyle. So, for example, no perching bird has webbed feet, and no duck or gull has great talons such as birds of prey have. Simply very clever variations on a theme.
Mr A. Atkinson
High Barnes, Sunderland.

When a bird is relaxed, its claws are naturally in a gripping position (the opposite to our hands). Therefore the bird will automatically hold onto the perch whilst sleeping, with no fear of falling off.
J. Belorgey
Hove, Sussex.

Sleeping birds do not fall off their perch on account of the bird bending its legs when relaxed.

The more the leg muscles relax the tighter the feet grasp the perch, due to muscles pulling the tendons. The tendons are connected to the toes which are rough so that the bird still has a tight grip until it wakes up and straightens its legs.
Roger Bolden
Chelmsford, Essex.

They stick to their perches mainly for the same reason why I can't remove their muck off my windscreen!
Sharon Barnes
Oxford.

I own a white car and it seems to attract more bird droppings than the other non-white cars I've owned. Is it my imagination or is there a scientific basis for this?

Birds can certainly distinguish certain colours, mainly for feeding and display, but there is no scientific evidence that a bird's choice of toilet location is selected chromatically.

However, there is ample circumstantial evidence that birds have phenomenal bowel control, being able to time and target their droppings to coincide with hanging out washing, cleaning windows, polishing cars etc.
Derek Niemann
Royal Society for the
Protection of Birds
Sandy, Bedfordshire.

There is a scientific basis for this: firstly, white is the most popular car colour, with red in second place.

Secondly, droppings show up more on white cars, whereas red is a very good colour for disguising dirt.
Kevin Jones
Coventry.

As far as I am aware there has been no statistical study conducted on this most interesting of subjects. However it is my feeling that perhaps it is possible that the light colour of the car is an attractant and may even have a startling effect on a bird, or certain types of bird, thus causing your unfortunate problem.
Marian Mowbray
Uxbridge.

In the 1950's, my house was directly beneath a bombing range used exclusively by seagulls. My car had a white roof and my neighbours' vehicles didn't. Sorties were pressed home with commendable accuracy, the majority of deliveries finding the white roof, with only minimal impact on the bonnet and the boot. The cars of the others were spared.

In a controlled experiment I exchanged parking positions with my neighbours either side, each a distance of some 30 yards away. In every case the effect was an instant adjustments of bombsights so that, while the other cars stayed clean, the white-roofed one copped the lot.

Ned Wilde
Crewkerne, Somerset.

Birds are extremely clean creatures and frightfully embarrassed that there are no public toilet facilities for them so, when inland, they search for places where the evidence of their embarrassment is the least obvious. Hence white cars, (and panama hats) but unfortunately, during the summer, they do not seem to be aware of the results of high diet of blackcurrants and other similar fruits.

T. M. Corrigan
Buxton, Derbyshire.

CASPARED?

Why does getting into the bath always trigger off the doorbell?

Dogs vary greatly in size and shape, yet they appear to know even from a distance, what is a dog and what is not a dog - how is this?

The eye level of a dog is different to ours, or to that of larger animals, such as horses. Since only other dogs and cats are likely to be frequently seen within this range of vision at a distance before that vision becomes very blurred, the dog is unlikely to be confused visually between other relatively small animals on the one hand, and humans and horses on the other. But some breeds of dogs may have short-sighted and quite blurred vision (as well as being largely colourblind), and these breeds may rely more upon smell to distinguish between dogs, cats, and humans at a distance.

It should be borne in mind that the dog has a sense of smell about a million times more powerful than our own. However, a dog which has encountered a cat within its 'formative period' of between four and fourteen weeks may thereafter be able to distinguish between a dog and a cat by movement alone. Otherwise a painful period of experimentation may be necessary before the dog realises that a cat is behaviourally a very different creature.

P.J. Cook
Walsall, West Midlands.

Anyone who has had their leg 'attacked' (for want of a better word) by a dog would argue that this isn't the case!

Ms M. J. Carr
Heysham, Lancashire.

Why is the worst damage to the ozone layer above the uninhabited Antarctic and not above the industrialised world?

With all the CFC's etc. discharged into the atmosphere above the industrialised world it does not take long for them to migrate from the troposphere to the stratosphere where an ozone-destroying reaction takes place.

The winds then sweep in a circular pattern around the pole and the stratosphere is isolated inside a vortex. The very low temperatures at high altitude stabilise ice particles in the clouds and these act as sites for a chemical reaction. So in the spring sunlight it produces an abundant new source of chlorine atoms in the Antarctic stratosphere causing a decrease in ozone that lasts through the year.

Mr B.K. Watts
Aspley, Nottingham.

CFC's are equally distributed around the world once in the upper atmosphere. However, CFC's on their own do not destroy the ozone layer. Certain clouds known as stratospheric aerosol clouds are able to transform CFC's into chlorine compounds capable of destroying ozone. These clouds only occur naturally at the two poles and above volcanic eruptions.

George Igler
London NW1.

It is known that the earth is hollow with the entrances to vast underworld kingdoms being in the vicinity of the poles. It is from these that pollution escapes, and as they are more industrialised, they ruin the ozone layer above them a lot quicker.

Mr C. Kershaw
Royton, Oldham.

Once they have used the legs what do restaurants do with the rest of the frog?

The answer according to a good French friend of mine, is that after the frog's leg and thigh is eaten there is only the head and a little skin left as waste.
Liz Rowntree
Newton Hall, Durham.

They make 'Toad in the Hole', and if this is wrong I'll be hopping mad!
Patricia Cardew
London.

They send them to the spawn shop.
L. Damiens
Southampton.

In restaurants after they have used the frogs' legs, the remainder is made into 'CROAKETTES'.
Des Sturges
Taunton, Somerset.

In Europe, I believe that the frogs are killed quite humanely, but in the East, from where many frogs' legs are now imported, the legs are just chopped off the living frog. The remainder of the unfortunate creature is then left to die slowly.
Rosemary Bennett
Frampton, Dorset.

After their defeat by England in the quarter finals of the Rugby World Cup, I should think they'll be dragged off to the Guillotine.
It does seem a bit harsh, however. Just refusing to serve them would have been sufficient punishment.
John Lindley
Sheffield.

Why don't birds get electrocuted when they perch on overhead power cables?

Two birds sat on a power line,
    that spanned from home to
    pylon;
One said, 'Why don't I get a
    shock? My claws aren't
    made of nylon!'
The other bird, a wise old owl,
    thought deeply on the
    query:
'I can answer your question,
    but you must learn electric
    theory.'
The mains contains 3 wires,
    the neutral, earth and live;
If you should touch the earth
    then you would certainly
    survive.
At each sub-power station,
    the neutral wire is bound
To a sturdy metal plate which
    is embedded in the ground.
So if you should touch the
    neutral, you will not burn
    your hand
For the neutral wire is
    grounded and your feet still
    touch the land.
The live wire is the one which

to touch could leave you
    dead
That is why it's colour-coded
    with the danger-colour, red;
But look at any gadget which
    requires power to work it
It must have at least two
    wires, or it will not make a
    circuit.
So if you should touch the
    live, your hand will feel
    quite sore
For the power finds a circuit
    through your body to the
    floor.
So to come back to the
    question; Why do birds not
    get a shock
When the power lines are
    covered by a large
    migrating flock?
The birds are safe as long as
    on a single wire they group
For they must first touch two
    conductors to complete a
    current loop
This shows why mice can run
    along the underground's

live rail,
They won't be electrocuted if
to close the loop they fail.
Said the owl, 'Now you
appreciate why you can
perch upon the line,
Touch no other wire nor the
ground and you will be just
fine.
The danger for the human is,
the neutral's linked to earth
At first sight this seems silly,
but the scheme does have
its worth.
Put a circuit in a metal box,
then connect the case to
ground;
If the live should touch the
casing then the fuse blows,
safe and sound.'
'Why, thank you!' said the
younger bird, and flew off
with elation;
The owl went happily to
sleep: he'd solved a
Tormentation.
Gareth Leyson
Keble College, Oxford.

If we could jump onto the
cable in the same way as
birds we would survive. We
would, like birds, charge up
instantly to the voltage of the
cable, but the electrical
current involved would be so
insignificant that we would
not even feel it.

If, however, we climbed the
metal pylon and put a foot or
hand on the cable, a huge
electrical current would flow
from the cable through our
bodies to the pylon and earth
and we would be killed. The
same applies then to birds,
and some pylon-roosting
large birds have been
electrocuted because of this.
Reg J. Baldwin,
Eastbourne, Sussex.

They have a claws in their
contract protecting them
from being over charged.
Tony Michielson,
Warwick.

CASPARED?

Why is it that when they
have all that grass to play
on, cricketers still prefer to
play on the scrubby bit in
the middle?

FACT!

Sauerkraut Day is
celebrated every year in
Wishek, North Dakota.

What happens if a cow doesn't get milked?

A cow produces milk only after the birth of a calf and in natural circumstances would continue to produce milk for that calf for about 300 days. In order to provide milk for human consumption the dairy cow has her calf taken away soon after birth and she is then milked by machine for the same period.

If no one milked the cow, she would have a tight, uncomfortable udder for a day or two and then dry up, the milk in her udder being re-absorbed into the body. This is much the same as what would happen in a wild situation if her calf either died or stopped feeding because of illness or accident.

Mrs Pat Maycock
Maynards Green, Sussex.

In the farming community this would be regarded as an 'udder' disaster!

Debbie Webster,
Ashbourne, Derbyshire.

What happens depends on what stage of lactation the animal is in (lactation being the length of milking period between calvings). If the cow is in peak or high production it will contract mastitis and then clinical mastitis. If this were to go untreated, it would possibly prove fatal, or at best the cow would lose all four drinking quarters.

If a cow is not milked in the lower end of milk production, there is less risk of mastitis and the cow will 'dry itself off' (milk production will stop).

Mrs Vanessa Bath
Winchester.

If you forget to milk your cow, the milk supply dries up after a few days. If she is a high yielding cow, mastitis, septicaemia, and other complications usually set in leaving you with, at best, a big vet's bill, or at worst, a bill from the knacker's yard.

H. Paterson
Upper Auchenlay,
Perthshire.

The theory is that all cows are either always milked or else they have a calf to drink the milk. Never in the whole experience of time and existence has a cow either not been milked or else had a calf except for one occasion.

This of course is on the one occasion in another time and universe where one cow was not milked. The udders unfortunately got bigger and bigger and bigger and ultimately got so phenomenally large that they exploded with the most incredible force.

Scientists are examining this as one of the theories behind the bang.
*Michelle Milsum
Edgware, Middlesex.*

If snow is comprised of water why is it white and not clear?

Snow is water that has crystallised and if it were examined on a microscopic level would appear to be clear.

The reason snow looks white is that the snow crystals have numerous small facets that reflect and scatter light. White light from the sun is therefore reflected from the snow and appears to us to be white (snow would appear to be red if it were illuminated with a red lamp).

On the same level refined sugar appears to be white when in the bowl but when examined more closely as individual grains is clear. This phenomenon is apparent also in many other surfaces such as shattered windscreens which appear white from a distance but are see-through from close up and waterfalls, toilet flushes, waves etc.
Gary Nichols
Horsham, West Sussex.

Actually it is neither. On close scrutiny snow will appear pale blue, the same as a still body of water reflecting the sky.
Victor Tabrizifar
Peterborough.

The real reason why snow is white and not clear is to hide the passing through the air of the Snow Queen in her ice chariot, partly because she has no clothes on and partly because if mortals caught sight of her it would be bad for them.
Mr P. E. Taylor
Birmingham.

CASPARED?

Why do people always ask you if you are all right if you fall over, when it is obvious you are not?

CHAPTER
EIGHT

A DAY IN THE LIFE

If we have to wear seatbelts in cars and planes, why don't we have to wear them on trains?

Have you ever tried wearing a seatbelt standing up!
Rebecca Openshaw
Walton on Thames.

All passengers on a plane must have a seat. Car passengers have no physical choice but to sit down. In contrast, train passengers feel a seat of their own is a bonus and obviously shouldn't be restricted.
Dianna Piercy
West Clandon, Surrey.

Who needs seat belts? It seems to me that the amount of chewing gum on the seats should be sufficient to keep passengers in place should the train actually be on time to crash.
M.L. Bourke
South Yardley, W. Midlands.

The forward momentum of the entire vehicle is so large that the telescoping or over-riding of the train on impact becomes the major consideration. It may actually be preferable to be thrown clear.
Nick Warren
Greenford, Middlesex.

Who ever heard of a train going fast enough that passengers needed to protect themselves with seatbelts?
Mr A. Parker
Yateley, Hants.

Because you are supposed to let the train take the strain.
Mr W. Crisp
New Eltham, London.

Where does household dust come from and why does most of it seem to be attracted to the TV?

Household dust is composed of various materials which are small and light enough to become airborne. Dust inside the house is produced mainly from our skin which is being constantly shed. Many DIY activities also help to produce dust. This is most obvious when sanding, sawing, mixing cement, and drilling. Clothes, footwear, and carpets also produce dust as they become worn. The hole in the elbow of your pullover contained material which could now be dust. Also, fine soil and mineral particles from outside the house may be blown in via doors and windows.

Colour television sets use voltages in excess of 20,000 volts to power the cathode ray tube. This causes a strong electrostatic field across the entire screen which continually attracts airborne dust. Much of this dust will remain on the screen even after the set is switched off. If you hold your arm close to the TV screen you will feel the hairs stand up as they are attracted by the field.
Allan Jackson
Purley, Surrey.

The questioner says most dust is attracted to the TV; my wife says I am. Two myths I'd like to explode.

Dust is made up of fine particles of earth, pollen, cloth, skin, etc, and, of course, can be attracted by heat. Although TV is undoubtedly a hot property, look under the bed, on top of doors or window ledges - even more dust!

The fact that the questioner sees most dust on TV is because, probably, like my wife she watches the set and not the programmes.
Alf Dewdney
Hayes, Middlesex.

Why are most dusters yellow?

The yellow flag flown on ships when free from infection is known as the yellow duster, could it derive from this?
Mrs Joy Seygrove
Tilbury, Essex.

This is probably because the wax polish used in Victorian and later days right up to my own youth and middle age was yellow. The dusters were not so likely to show ugly stains and make the housewife look as though she had done a substandard job of washing out the wax after use.
Eileen Denham
Chatham, Kent.

FACT!

The first ever successful heart transplant used the heart of a woman implanted into a man.

Most dusters are yellow because specks of dirt are more easily seen against a yellow background.
A black duster is just as efficient.
Michael Flynn
Whitley Bay.

While researching Christ's Hospital buttons, I found a reference to an instruction issued in 1636 that the children's clothes be 'dyed with a yellow couller'. Later, on 23 January 1638, the reason was given, 'to avoid vermin by reason the white cottons is held to breed the same'. Consequently, the yellow colour of dusters traditionally perpetuates the idea of cleanliness.
Gillian Meredith
The Button Museum
Ross on Wye.

The use of a strong yellow dye in dusters is the brainchild of an early textile researcher who realised that occasionally men are left to do the wash and that there was a good chance that they would include the dusters in the batch. This would result in a clothing catastrophe and therefore the necessity to replace the yellowed clothes. The restocking of clothes would benefit the textile industry in general and increase profits.

Mr G. Birch
St Leonards on Sea
East Sussex.

I would have thought dusters were yellow so as to distinguish them from other materials i.e. underwear.

Mrs N. Sanders
Great Sutton, South Wirral.

Most dusters are yellow, not because it is the cheeriest colour for an otherwise cheerless task, but to coincide with the predominant colour of spring flowers. Thus, women can undertake the annual spring clean up, confident that they are as busy as bees collecting pollen dust.

Wilma Coghill
Gosforth, Tyne and Wear.

CASPARED?

If dreams only last for a few seconds, how come we always manage to wake up in the middle of them?

FACT!

Tonga once produced a stamp in the shape of a banana.

CASPARED?

Why do bird droppings always hit the windows, but never the wall?

Which is better for the environment, being buried or cremated?

In the early days of cremation in the UK, it was presented as the environmentally-friendly option, with the anti-burial slogan of 'keeping the land for the living'.

I would argue that nowadays cemeteries and churchyards help protect the land from the living, preventing land being used for development and often acting as a refuge for wildlife. Again in the early days of cremation, the body was taken out of its coffin before being incinerated; nowadays, however, the coffins are all wastefully burnt and we are in the realms of European regulations concerning the pollution of the atmosphere and ground water from the glues used, and from the heavy metals, hydrochloric acid, carbon dioxide, sulphur dioxide and hydrofluoric acid in the emissions. Already there has had to be a ban on cremating bodies that are wearing rubber soled shoes.

Groups such as the Natural Death Centre are trying to promote the concept of green and 'DIY' funerals; these could include burials at sea with the body placed in a simple shroud; cardboard coffins similar to those available in the States; reusable coffins, plus biodegradable body bags. My own favourite option is burial not too deep for anaerobic action, with a fruit tree planted on top, resulting in memorial orchards, with each tree carefully tended by the family concerned, to complement the government's planned new 'community forests'.
Nicholas Albery
London.

Both, if it's your mother-in-law. Just to be sure!
E.H.T. Islip
St. Leonards on Sea.

Why can you get the top off a tube of superglue?

Superglue is a cyanoacrylate adhesive, incapable of bonding the plastic from which its tube and/or cap are made.

Cyanoacrylates also have an Achilles heel, shearing stress; this is the type of stress applied when the cap is turned relative to the tube. And like most other fluid adhesives, while in a capped container they are virtually isolated from air and, lacking a reagent or catalyst, remain fluid.

J.M.G. Eadie
Leeds.

FACT!

The Great Red Spot on the planet Jupiter is about three times the size of our Earth.

FACT!

Although we use the expression 'to sweat like a pig', it is a fact that pigs don't sweat.

FACT!

The first potato crisp is believed to have been invented by a Red Indian by the name of George Crum.

FACT!

One of the major causes of fire in the United States is due to electrical cables being eaten by rats.

If I built a car, say a Mini, entirely out of spares, would it be cheaper than buying one from a dealer?

Some years ago I worked for Vauxhall Motors in their Parts Division Export Section. A South American dealer's son then living in London approached the company with a project to build a car for competing in inter-dealership races in British Guyana. Rather than strip an existing vehicle down and upgrade its performance, chucking away hosts of expensive but unnecessary trim and bits, he decided to buy it in parts form. The vehicle was to be assembled in a small mews garage before being shipped abroad.

This was a horrendous task, not just identifying all the components, as there are thousands in a car, but also gathering them together for delivery to the customer. Just a few out of stock vital bits could have fouled up the whole venture. Added to this was the required knowledge and many specialised skills needed to make a car. Unlike Airfix models, there are no manuals on actually how to self-build a production car, save those references used by the manufacturing plant itself, and these are unlikely to be available at the local library.

The main crunch comes in costing the enterprise. In most cases, more profit is made by the makers from selling parts for the cars, rather than on the actual finished models themselves. Even buying such a large quantity of components in one consignment and enjoying top discounts, it still works out much more expensive. That's without considering the amount of

time the assembly would take, the overheads of premises, and the cost of the necessary equipment. It is probably a lot easier just to buy a new car.
Peter Hughes
Cornwall.

I used to work in the Part Department with British Leyland many years ago and have heard of two instances where people have, as an experiment, priced all the individual parts together for a Mini and a Morris 1000. In both cases the price of the individual parts came to about three times the price of the completed car. In the case of the Mini the showroom price at the time was about £1,500 and the cost of the individual parts came to over £4,000. So it does seem that to get value for money it is best to buy a completed car from the showroom.
Keith Robson
Doncaster, South Yorkshire.

Yes, it would: I've done it. I built a Mini using a shell and spares from other Minis and it took me approximately two years. It worked out slightly cheaper than buying one; however, in time, sweat, tears, and blood, it cost a whole lot more (and my girlfriend has only just started talking to me again).
Ian Stock
St. Albans, Herts.

I've had so much trouble with my new one, I'm convinced the makers are already doing it!
Robert Shaw
Bristol.

FACT!

In medieval Japan it was a sign of beauty to have black teeth.

FACT!

It is easier to catch a cold from shaking hands than from kissing.

Why do dark drinks like Guinness always have a white froth?

The froth has been devised by breweries as an optical aid for novice drinkers, enabling them, at a glance, to determine where to begin drinking thus causing them no embarrassment when in the company of more ardent professionals.
Mr J. Knowles,
Wavertree, Liverpool.

Dark drinks need a white head so that in dimly lit pubs or restaurants you can see that you have got a drink, where it is and how much is left in the glass.
Lorene Ross
London.

Froth consists of numerous tiny bubbles which are so thin as to be virtually transparent. Light falling on these bubbles is thoroughly 'mixed up' by reflections and refraction (bending). This makes it impossible to see through the froth, or to see a reflection, as you can with a large single bubble. White light reflected in the froth gives the impression of whiteness and in a dark drink such as Guinness 'appears' to be the opposite colour of what it actually is.
David Todd,
South Woodford, London.

FACT!

The bicycle was invented only 23 years before the first motor car.

FACT!

Canada has enough lakes to fit the whole of the British mainland in them three times.

Why do most countries have plug sockets with two holes and yet we have sockets with three?

British sockets have holes giving provision for a plug earth pin to cater for appliances that need to be earthed. The facility is there regardless as to whether the earth pin of the plug is used. All countries have sockets with provision for earthing, but in some cases these are not in common use.

In continental Europe, there are many types of socket. The common French socket has an earth pin, and two holes for the pins which carry the current. The standard German socket is recessed and has side contacts for earthing purposes and only two holes for the current-carrying pins of the plug.

Earthing is not needed for double insulated appliances which are now prevalent and generally have a low current consumption and some countries make sockets with two holes and no earthing facility to cater specifically for these appliances.

Conrad Edel
London.

In this country we have a higher voltage (220/240V) which is sufficient to cause death should a person be electrocuted; in other countries the current is generally much lower at 110V, which is regarded as being considerably less of a danger. We therefore had to think of safety features earlier and plumped for a method of earthing through means of a third pin. On the continent the need for a third pin (earth) was not so great and they maintained the two pin system. Only later did they begin to use an earthing system through the plug, but adapted it for a two pin plug.

Mr E.J. Baker
Bath, Avon.

Why are dinner plates round?

The answer is simple, it is a thousand times easier making a round plate on a potter's wheel than a square one.
Miss K. Carr
Ashton in Makerfield,
Wigan.

If plates were not round you would not be able to chase your peas round them, and considering this is one of Britain's most popular pastimes no plate manufacturer would dare make plates any other shape for fear of losing customers.
Mrs J.M. Ball
Ilkley, West Yorkshire.

Forget aesthetics, the
  potter's wheel,
They're not what shapes the
  perfect meal.
The answer, if you want the
  true one:
If plates are round you get
  more food on!
J. Hand,
Chichester, West Sussex.

In 1482 Leonardo da Vinci envisaged the basic concept of the microwave oven. Concerned that square plates would interfere with the rotation of the turntable he proposed that plates should therefore be round. His ideas were met with derision from his peers and he lived out his life as an idealistic fool until his death in 1519. How embarrassed they would be now to see that, as with the helicopter, da Vinci's vision was, in fact, to come true.
Graham Jones
Great Eccleston, Lancashire.

Dinner plates are usually round due to something called 'health'. A round plate has no corner in which particles and germs could not be easily accessible. Any other shaped plate would have corners and therefore potential health risks attached.
Ms S. Howett
Gateshead, Tyne and Wear.

Why do we use a red carpet for VIPs?

We have a red carpet for VIPs so that it won't show the bloodstains if they are assassinated.
D. Thorp
Fallowfield, Manchester.

In approximately the 6th century BC red dye was obtained by crushing sea shells, called Murniex, or shellfish (Porphyria), in Ancient Greece.
In order to produce a small quantity of dye a large amount of them had to be crushed, which obviously made them very expensive. To have the colour red was regarded as a symbol of great wealth and importance.
Miss V. R. Conner
Sherfield on Loddon, Hants.

The actual carpet is simply a mark of courtesy and respect shown by the provision of a pleasant surface to walk on. The colour red is the central thing. Red, in British tradition, signifies importance and dignity.
'Red Books' (books bound in red) are used for court guides; peerage lists; directories of state servants, and official regulations.
The 'Red Box' is a minister's red covered box for official documents.
Red hatbands are still worn by senior army officers to indicate their distinctive rank.
'Red letter' days we still celebrate.
It seems that everything important needs red - simple!
Mrs V. Thwaites
London SE17.

The reason we use a carpet stems from the ancient ritual of maidens placing flower petals in the path of kings, emperors and gods etc. These days it is far more cost effective to purchase a re-usable if somewhat expensive plush red carpet than to line the pockets of the local florists.
Peggy McCloud
Stevenston, Ayrshire.

We are always told to put our valuables in the car boot. But why don't thieves break into car boots?

Thieves do try to break into car boots, but it seems most of them get caught in the act. Hence the large number of trapped fingers seen in the back of most vehicles.
Kimberley Thomas Tamworth, Staffs.

Thieves do indeed break into car boots. However, thieves are, in the main opportunists, and steal items which they can see and which they either fancy for themselves or know they can dispose of.

Thus items in the boot, which are, of course, out of sight, are less vulnerable. Furthermore, prior to the development of the hatchback, the boot of a car was easily the most secure part (steel is many times stronger than standard autoglass). Unfortunately, however, when most hatchbacks are entered (e.g. via a window or door) the boot area is readily accessible.

I would advise all motorists not to leave valuables in the car at all. If they must do so for short periods, the advice to put them in the boot, out of sight, still holds good.
Chief Inspector J.J. Vernon South Yorkshire Police.

The reason us tea leaves don't break into car boots guv is 'cos it's a case of 'out of sight out of mind' innit? If you leave the gear in the motor we can see what's worth nicking but we'd draw an awful lotta blanks if we took pot luck with car boots wouldn't we? Life's too short guv - know what I mean?
Clive 'Fingers' Whichelow London.

Why are all the letters on a typewriter arranged in the way they are, rather than simply from A to Z?

The 'QWERTY' keyboard was introduced by the inventor of the first commercially successful typewriter, C. Latham Sholes, in 1873. It was designed to slow the typist so that the relatively crude mechanism did not keep on jamming and despite improvements in typewriter mechanisms it has remained popular.

The chief rival to the Sholes layout was the Calligraph keyboard, but a speed typing competition in 1877 proved that 'QWERTY' was superior in both speed and ease of use. The only other major rival was designed by Dr August Dvorak in 1932. He claimed that his layout could increase typing speeds by up to 35 per cent. Unfortunately it never really caught on although it is available as an optional extra for computers.
David Skinner
Wilford, Nottingham.

The letters on a typewriter are arranged the way they are so that the most commonly used letters are positioned to give the maximum speed to the typist with the minimum of effort. The most common keyboard is the 'QWERTY' - derived from the first six letters, top row, from left to right. In a competitive world, typists have had the letters on their keyboards arranged to suit their individual needs to give them their fastest speeds.
Lee Adams
Neath, West Glamorgan.

This system was first devised so that all the letters of the word 'TYPEWRITER' could be found on the top line. This was supposedly to assist inexperienced salespeople demonstrate the typewriter.
D. J. Erskine
Newbury, Berkshire.

What are the health risks of keeping the top of a photocopying machine up when you are operating it?

Beyond causing slight eye strain, using my photocopier with its lid up for many years has resulted in no damage to my health.

However, there are some good reasons pertaining to the health of one's machine that make it sensible to use it with the lid down.

Constant use with the lid up causes the light sensitive mechanics inside the machine to wear out faster in addition to encouraging dirt to accumulate within the machine. Not only that but having the lid up will cause the machine to use up more of the black powder or toner at a faster rate.

It is in the interests of the user's pocket and not necessarily his health therefore to close the lid.
D.J. Reece
Horwich, Bolton.

There is a definite health risk involved in this practice. In my experience most injuries occur to hands and are caused by someone slamming the lid down on them at the same time shrieking very loudly 'My God, you mustn't do that it's terribly bad for you!' Additional and associated risks involved are perforated eardrums from the shrieking, and associated shock.
Susan Ormond
Burghfield Common,
Reading.

The health risks are mainly that :
you'll feel light headed,
you'll feel light headed,
you'll feel light headed,
you'll feel light headed...
John Vance
Auchtermuchty, Fife.

Given incomparable costs in technology, production, and transportation, why is petrol six times more expensive than beer?

People commonly buy petrol five or more gallons at a time, but buy beer by the pint. Thus beer is at least forty times more expensive to dispense.
Bob Hewitt,
Wigan, Lancs.

A major cost of both beer and petrol is the tax imposed on them. Once the basic infrastructure such as oil refineries, derricks, etc are in place, oil which is available for 'free' in the oil rich nations can be cheaply pumped-up and converted into petrol in the millions of gallons. Beer is produced on a vastly smaller scale and requires labour intensive conversion of hops through several stages to make the final product. Hops have to be grown on valuable land, farmers have to be paid etc, unlike oil which is already there and the much larger quantity involved means each unit can be produced at a much cheaper price.
Antony Socrates
Westbourne, Bournemouth.

Beer is more expensive than petrol owing to the higher rate of tax on it. The cost of beer has no knock-on effect on inflation and is thus a popular target for the Chancellor. Design an engine that could run on beer and you'll get cheaper drinking.
Tim Hopkins
Luton, Beds.

The reason is simple, most beers taste appreciably better than petrol. Real ales are also more environmentally friendly than super unleaded.
John Aspray
Lychett Matravers, Dorset.

Should you keep eggs in the fridge?

Eggs are best kept at room temperature otherwise they will crack when immersed in boiling water. It is for this reason that most people put a little salt in the water when boiling eggs.

If you do insist on putting eggs in the fridge, my only suggestion is that you remove them at least thirty minutes before boiling.
Audrey Ramsey
Braunston, Northants.

On health grounds the answer is *yes*.

If an egg happens to contain the salmonella bacteria, then keeping it at an ambient temperature provides the optimum conditions for bacterial growth.

Eggs should be kept at a temperature between 3 and 6 degrees Celsius as this inhibits the growth of any bacteria that may be present.
Stephen Rego
Royal Gwent Hospital,

Eggs should be stored in a cool place such as a cold larder that is not too dry. They should be kept away from strong flavours as eggs are easily 'flavour affected'. If stored correctly, eggs will normally remain in good condition for two to three weeks, and can be checked for freshness by placing in water. If it is fresh it will sink.
Jane Beston
Tonbridge, Kent.

Eggs are porous and keeping them cool helps to stop moisture evaporating from them and maintains their freshness. Kept in their box in a fridge is ideal, as this further reduces evaporation and stops eggs from picking up odours from other foods. Eggs should be stored with the pointed end down as the yolk rises and the air sac, which is at the rounded end of an egg, cushions the yolk and reduces contact with the porous shell.
Jo Rimmer
London.

Why are 20p pieces smaller than 10p pieces?

If the value of coins were to be related to size, one would need a magnifying glass to see a 5p, and a microscope for the 2p and 1p pieces.
I.G. Hughes
Stroud, Gloucestershire.

For economy and convenience, newly introduced coins and notes are smaller sized. The 10p piece has remained unaltered because of its nationwide use in coin-operated machines, notably the telephone call-boxes.
J.A. Deamer
Faversham, Kent.

The same question could be asked comparing £1 coins with 50p pieces, or 1p pieces with 5p pieces. Might I suggest that it is not the size of coins that matters but the weight and shape of them. This is so that blind people can determine their value by feeling them.
Leo Appleton
Southport.

If coins increased in size in relation to their value, 50p and £1 coins would have to be carried in backpacks.
Peter J. Thompson
Bangor, N. Ireland.

The 10p was first issued in 1968 with a diameter of 28mm. This was the same size as the old florin as they were worth the same, £1/10. The florin had not changed size since 1887, when it was a silver coin. The 20p was issued much later, in 1982, with a diameter of 21mm. It was made smaller because a 'slot' was needed that was practical and a coin twice the size of the 10p would have been too big.

Instead it was given a different shape and thickness to make it stand out.

Even the new, smaller 10p issued this year will be larger than the 20p (24.5mm), and heavier.
Richard Coxon
Mickleover, Derby.

Can recycled paper be recycled?

Yes! Recycled fibres can be recycled approximately 4 to 6 times. Waste paper represents 53 per cent of fibre used in the production of UK paper and board utilised mainly in the packaging and newspaper sectors.

Recycled paper however is not suitable for every application, nor can paper be recycled indefinitely as the fibres become shorter and weaker and lose the necessary paper making qualities. Virgin woodpulp will therefore always be required to ensure that quality is maintained.

Kathy Bradley
Paper Information Bureau
Westlea, Swindon.

Everything in the Universe including paper can be recycled and recycled again. Just take a look at any evening's entertainment on the television and the radio programme listings.

A. Sutton
Oldham, Lancashire.

Paper fibres start as long fibres with a high strength, but break into smaller lengths each time it is recycled, reducing the strength of the paper. This is counteracted to a limited extent by the addition of various chemicals to increase the final strength. The main cost determining the number of times paper can be recycled is the processing needed to remove the impurities added each time it is used, i.e. inks, glues, dyes etc.

When paper is no longer suitable to be recycled as paper it can be used to make compost and soil conditioners, returning it to where it came from to grow more trees, thus starting the whole process again.

Mr J. P. Royle
Nottingham.

In the case of toilet paper I certainly hope not!

David Stroud
Ipswich, Suffolk.

Why don't teabags disintegrate?

Teabag paper is made from two strong fibres, manila hemp, a natural fibre (used to make rope) for strength, and thermoplastic fibres, to seal the bags. The two fibres are not woven together, they are laid down as a watery mixture in two separate layers. They form paper when the water drains away and the damp web remaining is squeezed dry through rollers. The resulting paper has pores varying in size which let boiling water in, but are small enough to stop any tea leaves escaping.
Julian Raithby,
Southminster, Essex.

Because they are able to take the strain!
Alan Leadbetter
Alcester, Warwickshire.

It must be because they are 'tea-total'.
Jean Strong
Dorchester, Dorset.

FACT!

The first song played on music station MTV when it started in 1981 was *Video Killed The Radio Star* by the Buggles.

FACT!

Winston Churchill won the Nobel Prize for Literature in 1953 for his book *Saurola*.

FACT!

The bell known as Big Ben at the Houses of Parliament weighs 13 tons and has a crack in it.

Why do cakes that are stale go hard, while biscuits that are stale go soft?

Cakes are baked to retain a fairly high degree of moisture, making them nice to eat. When they are a few days old some moisture will have evaporated and they then go dry and hard. Biscuits are baked to have a very low residual moisture content, and unless they are kept in an airtight tin then they absorb moisture, which makes them soft.

Iain McWhinnie
Dalgety Bay, Fife.

The longer you keep a cake waiting for the knife, the more tense (thus hard) it gets; while biscuits go soft at the prospect of being dunked in hot liquid!

Ron Farley
Selby, North Yorkshire.

One difference between cakes and biscuits is the fact that cakes are cooked longer. This hardens the fat in cakes (by increasing the number of hydrogen bonds and making the fat more saturated). Once the natural moisture of the cake has evaporated you are left with what it essentially is, a hardened product. Biscuits are only cooked for 15 to 20 minutes. The fat is less hardened and can revert to its original state which is soft at room temperature. It is fat rather than water which accounts for biscuits going soft. Also cakes contain eggs where biscuits are less likely to; eggs are a further source of saturated (i.e. hard) fat with no moisture retaining properties.

A. G. Pitt
Cardiff.

When using cooking foil should I keep the shiny side on the outside or the inside?

In theory it is better to use the bright side of the foil against the food due to the foil's reflective properties. However, in practice, the difference is so very slight when cooking conventionally, that it really does not matter which side of the foil is used.
Paul Ruocco
Marketing Manager
British Alcan
Amersham, Bucks.

CASPARED?

The world is divided into time zones that run from west to east but all converge at the poles. If so, what time is it at the north pole?

FACT!

A typical kiss burns up about 3 calories.

FACT!

In 1957 the Grand National was run on a Friday instead of its traditional Saturday.

FACT!

The first actress ever to appear on a stamp was Grace Kelly.

FACT!

Cliff Richard had 17 top ten hits before the Beatles even got into the charts.

How do the police estimate crowds?

The police estimate crowds by using the probability method. They look back through past figures and conditions and they can take an average or work out how much land there is available and the likelihood of the area being filled by using other figures for the same circumstances. The estimates are normally quite accurate although there is always an exception to the rule.

Catherine Woods
Thorpe Bay, Essex.

They estimate the size of the crowd by multiplying the number of policemen available by ten.

Miss J.M. MacDonald
Bow, London.

Easy! They count the legs and divide by two. However, these estimates can be wildly inaccurate when dogs and one-legged people are present.

Angela Sabberton
Wroxham, Norfolk.

Crowds are estimated by experience. Knowing that there are 80,000 people at a Cup Final in Wembley or 30,000 at a full-house for a test match at the Oval, or the Odeon, Hammersmith holds 3,500. However, the Jacob Formula allows one person per 4 square feet (0.37m squared) tight crowd, to 9 and a half square feet (0.88m squared) loose crowd. Thus a tight crowd in Whitehall, London would be about 75,000 to 100,000 people. Accuracy is possibly plus or minus 10 to 15 per cent.

Anthony Phillips
London.

They wait for the organisers to announce their figures, then half it and, depending on the mood of the officer concerned, add or subtract a few so as not to look too obvious. These figures are normally as underestimated as the organisers' are overestimated.

Philip Sunter
Pudsey, West Yorkshire.

CHAPTER

NINE

PEOPLE AND PLACES

Where do people in hell tell each other to go?

They would probably say 'go to the Devil' to each other, while the big man himself would probably say 'you're fired'.
K. Hopkins
Stoke on Trent, Staffs.

Hell, being an Hermetic allegory for the unruly, conscious mind, it would, therefore, appear more appropriate for those dwelling in such a place (all of us) to tell one another to go somewhere more realistically tormenting, such as the dentist's, the House of Commons or Milton Keynes.
Mr I. Thomas
Stockton on Tees, Cleveland.

I would imagine they tell each other to watch reruns of Jeremy Beadle, with the cry 'Go to Bead-Hell'.
Andrew Jenkinson
Pocklington, York.

They obviously tell each other to go to blazes.
G.F. Malin
West Derby, Liverpool.

As somebody who has lived in Hell all her life I would most definitely tell people to go to Florida. However, for myself I would like to go to London and see Princess Diana and the Houses of Parliament!
Rose Ley
Hell General Store and Post Office
Hell, Michigan, USA.

Nobody in hell tells anybody where to go because hell is so full of perjuring police officers, thieving tycoons, bent barristers, perverted parsons, and corrupt cabinet ministers that there is quite simply no room to go anywhere.
R.C. Humphreys
Barnsley, South Yorkshire.

177

Where is the centre of the United Kingdom, based on the distribution of population?

Ideally, we should have to take the line of longitude which divided the population into two equal halves, east and west, and place it across the line of latitude which halved the population, north and south. The point of intersection would be the answer to our destination.

Unfortunately, this is very difficult to answer because the census of population is taken according to the irregular lines of county boundaries. However, if we take the populations of counties starting with the most southerly, Cornwall, and add them together, moving steadily northwards, we come to a line of counties which brings the total to 28,086,000 (just over half the population of the UK). If we now do the same running from east to west until we find about half the population we find that the two lines meet in roughly the central area for population. When I tried this test I found that the West Midlands is the fulcrum on which the two lines pivot. The centre of the spread of population therefore lies within this densely populated conurbation of over two and a half million people. It will be surprising if the figures for the 1991 census have any significant effect on this conclusion.

Incidentally, the geographical centre of England (not the UK) is reputed to be Meriden, a village also in the West Midlands.

Noel Blackham
Edgbaston, Birmingham.

One hears of the First and Third Worlds, but what or where is the Second World?

Sociologist Peter Worsley, the man generally thought to have first used the term Third World, avoided answering this question. There were two existing powers, the United States and the Communist Bloc, and hence those developing nations who were the Third World. The question of primacy between the two existing powers wasn't an issue.

J. Hand,
Chichester, West Sussex.

The Second World was composed of the Communist countries, mainly those in Eastern Europe, Cuba and China. For a while now this term, along with First and Third Worlds, has not been used, being replaced instead by developed and developing nations.

Miss J. Pugh
Solihull, West Midlands.

The 'Second World' in political and geographical terms are countries with industrialised centrally planned economies. Examples of this are getting fewer, but in the past, the USSR, much of Eastern Europe and currently North Korea. Interestingly enough, geographers also use other terms. The Fourth World refers to the poorest of the poor (Bhutan, Bangladesh etc) whilst the Fifth World refers to OPEC countries which have undergone rapid development because of their oil supplies.

Julian Sinclair
London.

CASPARED?

Why is it that whenever the doorbell goes, the dog always thinks it's for him?

Why are so many people named Jones in Wales, when there is no letter 'J' in the Welsh language?

The Welsh originally had a patronymic system of names. In the 16th and 17th centuries, the English system of fixed surnames, under which the son had the same surname as the father, was imposed as were English spellings of names. Thus Ifan ab Cwain might become Evan Owen (or Bowen or, occasionally, Owens). The name Sion, pronounced like Shone (which survives as a surname), was very common and was the Welsh equivalent of John. All the men whose fathers were named Sion ended up as Jones, John or Johns. The initial J was used because that was the letter which began the English name John, although the rest of the surname reflected the pronunciation of the Welsh name.

Ian Miller
Cardiff.

Long after the English began using permanent surnames the Welsh continued the practice of listing themselves by personal genealogy. They would describe themselves as so-and-so, son of so-and-so, son of so-and-so.

As Wales became English-dominated, the English found this system very awkward for tax-collecting purposes, so the bureaucrats of the time decided to impose surnames. Often this was done by anglicising Welsh Christian- or nick-names, but sometimes, when a scribe who knew no Welsh was confronted by a man who claimed his name was Dafydd ap Gerallt ab Ieuan Goch he would arbitrarily impose an English surname. One of the most common being 'Johns' which became corrupted to Jones.

P. Bevan
Prescot, Merseyside.

With all the money Nanette Newman makes from doing advertisements, why doesn't she own a dishwasher?

Let's FACE it, Nanette may be BUBBLY, GENTLE too, but she is neither SOFT nor GREEN!

She knows she can increase her LIQUID assets by advertising MILD detergent for washing large amounts of DISHES by HAND, not machine.

She would not want to tempt fate, in the form of her FAIRY Godmother by using a dishwasher.
Janet Burholt
Dorchester, Dorset.

Nanette Newman *does* own a dishwasher. An upright, very reliable model, works under its own steam so saving on electricity, is apt to be temperamental though if overloaded. Senior models can be converted for use to other mundane household chores. A very popular item, with millions of them having been produced.

The name of this user-friendly high tech model - the Husband!
J. R. Stock
Chichester, West Sussex.

Of course she owns a dishwasher, how do you think she keeps her hands so soft in the first place.
Miss X. Whitson,
Edinburgh.

The fact she is so rich means that she can go out to dinner every night and therefore has no washing up which would require a dishwasher.
Martha Brett
Colchester, Essex.

She might well make plenty of money doing ads, but she still can't afford a dishwasher because just count the number of kids she has to feed and clothe.
Mrs S. Eagles
Clacton on Sea, Essex.

Whatever happened to Frank Serpico, the New York cop who fought police corruption?

Serpico retired in 1972 and was awarded a medal for bravery. He then settled in Switzerland.
Mrs Irene Tapping
Totnes, Devon.

Serpico is now living in Dyfed, West Wales, near to the town of Haverfordwest. I take it he did not want to live in New York any more.
J. P. Anderson
London SW16.

After retiring from the New York police in 1972 I lived for a while in Switzerland and then embarked on a long travel of experience around the rest of Europe staying for a considerable time in Holland, and then North Wales where I worked at the Orissor College.

After my time in Europe I returned to North America and travelled extensively round Mexico, Canada, and the United States pursuing my various interests.

I now live in New York State in a 40 x 20 ft solar powered farmhouse and work as close to nature as possible. Age and the bullet still left in my head have not seriously affected me. In fact I feel healthier now than at any other point in my life. I put this down to holistic medicine and the art of Shiatsu. I keep myself busy by helping at the local animal shelter and by various writing projects. Thank you Britain for being so interested in my welfare.
Frank Serpico
New York State, USA.

FACT!

British citizens do not legally need a passport to return to the UK.

What was Billy Joe McAllister throwing off the bridge in the Bobbie Gentry song *Ode to Billy Joe*?

There have been lots of theories about what Billy Joe McAllister threw off the Tallahatchee bridge in Bobbie Gentry's 1967 hit *Ode to Billy Joe*. Some have included flowers, a ring, and even a baby. Bobbie Gentry who wrote, as well as sang the song, in interviews at the time of its success declined to give an answer, leaving the listener to make their own decision whilst also adding to the song's mystery. She said 'The song is a study in unconscious cruelty' and 'what was thrown off the bridge is not important but the nonchalant way the family talks about the (Billy Joe's) suicide'.

For those who continued to wonder the answer came in 1976 when a motion picture based on the song's lyrics was made starring Robby Benson and Glynnis O'Connor.

According to the film Billy Joe threw his girlfriend's rag doll Benjamin off the bridge and committed suicide the next day because he was unsure of his sexual preference.

To tie in with the film Bobbie Gentry re-recorded the song which charted briefly.

Mr T. Bailey
Bingham, Notts.

Billy Joe McAllister threw himself off the bridge probably after listening to too many maudlin country and western songs from the likes of Bobbie Gentry and Co.

Howard McGuigan
Bognor Regis, West Sussex.

What is the national costume of England?

We don't have one. This is obvious when in the Miss World contest, the English contestant ends up having to wear a Beefeater suit during the national dress section. Perhaps we are just too individual.
Catherine Ellis
Cranleigh, Surrey.

The national costume of England unlike that of many other nations has never stood still, but like its society has evolved through the ages. It now stands as: denim jeans, trainers and football shirts with regional variations.
Jeanette Green
Hornchurch, Essex.

Probably this season it will be the pin-striped suit, bowler hat and brolly for the upper classes and flat cap and donkey jacket for the working class. What the men will be wearing though, I've no idea.
Peter Critchworth
Darlington.

The costume that most evokes the spirit of the English is that of the shepherdess for the female, i.e., peasant blouse, three-quarter, panniered skirt, laced waistcoat, petticoat, stockings, buckled shoes and a bonnet. For the male it is that of the countryman, i.e., handmade full shirt, knee breeches, hose, buckled shoes, and a sleeveless coat.
Mrs H. M. Maynard
Guildford, Surrey.

Considering our abysmal climate, our national costume must be an anorak and wellies.
Sheila Guy
Great Barr, Birmingham.

Take a long look around your local village green, especially around 1 May time, and you may find our national costume is that of the Morris dancer.
Pat Sperring
Birchington, Kent.

184

Union Jack shorts and tattoos of either Love and Hate or Mum and Dad on each forearm or fingers.
Ainsley Best
St Helier,
Channel Islands.

We see the national dress each year in Spanish resorts. The 'Brit on Tour' wears string vest, knotted hanky and turned up trousers.
Ian Scott
Leith, Edinburgh.

What is Dr Who's first name?

Firstly, Who is not his surname. The series title is meant as a question: Dr Who? Who is he? Where does he come from? Consequently, he cannot have a first name, to match the surname he does not have.

In the 28 years since the series started we have never been told his real name. In the very first story, his would-be companions assumed that his surname was Foreman, as his granddaughter Susan had used this surname at the local Coal Hill school. He has indicated to us that his name would be too difficult for us to pronounce. In the story 'Remembrance of the Daleks', he did leave a calling card that was comprised of mathematical symbols. In 'Spearhead from Space' he did use the alias Dr John Smith, and has used this on a number of occasions. In 'The Happiness Patrol', he indicated that his nickname at college was Theta Sigma. And now with the series under considerable doubt, we may never know his real name.

Keith Andrews
Camberwell, London.

The principal character in *Doctor Who* is called the Doctor and not Doctor Who as many people believe. Therefore the Doctor has no Christian or surname. However, his real name is not the Doctor either; this is just something he likes to be called. The Doctor's real name is unpronounceable by humans and is in fact an alien mathematical equation. However, during his exile on Earth, the Doctor went by the name Doctor John Smith.

Guy Lambert
Nuneaton, Warwickshire.

Whatever happened to Sherpa Tensing?

I think that he is still on top of Mount Everest after losing his AA Route Map!
James Crobb
Chilcompton, nr Bath, Somerset.

Sherpa Tensing retired from expedition leading and set up a motor van factory.
Neil Huntington
Goole, North Humberside.

He came down and married Zebra Crossing.
Leslie Thomas
Southsea, Hampshire.

FACT!

Coronation Street was originally going to be called 'Florizel Street', but its name was changed at the last minute by the producers.

Sherpa Tenzing Norgay, the man who with Sir Edmund Hilary conquered Mount Everest on 29 May 1953, died in the Indian city of Darjeeling in May 1986 at the age of 72.

After his historic climb he was awarded the George Cross and the Star of Nepal. He then lived most of his life in the relative obscurity of an Indian hill station teaching climbing.

On his death, the then Prime Minister of India, Rajiv Gandhi, hailed him as 'the tiger of the snows', and said the whole nation would mourn his death.
David Embling
Bromley, Kent.

In '86 him pass away
Now Himalayan peace.
Janet Burholt
Dorchester, Dorset.

Whatever happened to the two stars of *Randall and Hopkirk (Deceased)*?

The answer to this question lies in an episode never shown in this country, or anywhere in the world for that matter.

Hopkirk had a bit of a bust up with Randall, and decided to teach him a lesson by tampering with the brake pipes on his car. Unfortunately, the resulting crash was far more serious than Hopkirk had anticipated, resulting in the programme having to be retitled *Randall & Hopkirk (Both Dead)*.

This led to a massive drop in viewing figures, and eventually the series was axed.

Mr R. Griffith
Birkenhead, Wirral.

Mike Pratt, who played Jeff Randall, appeared in many of the action and adventure series of the 1960's and 1970's both before and after *Randall and Hopkirk*, such as *The Saint*, *The Baron*, *The Champions*, and *Dangerman*. He was last seen in *The Brothers* which he was working on at the time of his death in July 1976.

Kenneth Cope, who played the late Marty Hopkirk, had made his name as Jed Stone in *Coronation Street*. He appeared in several *Carry On* films, and series such as *Catweazle*, *Minder* and *Doctor Who*. During the early 1980's he retired from acting, becoming a successful restaurateur. More recently he has returned to acting and has been seen in *City Lights*, *Truckers*, *Shelley*, and *The Bill*. He was last seen at the Belgrade theatre in Coventry in a play called *Safe in Our Hands*.

Matthew Newton
Storbridge, West Midlands.

We know who lives at Numbers 10 and 11, but who lives in the rest of Downing Street?

Number 10 Downing Street has been the official residence and official office of the British prime minister since 1735, when the house was accepted from King George II by Sir Robert Walpole in his official capacity as First Lord of The Treasury. The house is one of three in Downing Street which still remain from a street of houses built by Sir George Downing, who obtained the lease on the site, partly through Royal favour, in 1860. His other two surviving houses are No. 11, the official residence of the Chancellor of the Exchequer, and No. 12, the ground floor and basement of which are used as offices for the Government whips.
Dr Julian Daniels
Anlaby, Hull.

Apart from the Prime Minister at No. 10 and the Chancellor of the Exchequer at No. 11, there is only one other house on Downing St. No. 12 Downing Street is the official home of the Government Chief Whip, Richard Ryder, although he does not actually reside there.

The remainder of Downing Street is occupied by the Privy Council Offices.
Mrs S. A. McLaughlin
Glasgow.

No. 12 Downing Street is the home of the corner shop, selling all manner of food and drink until all hours of the night, so that if John Major comes home late from a sitting, Norma can pop next door for a bag of frozen chips and a can of beer.
Carol Youlton
Ashton under Lyne, Lancs.

Whatever happened to little Jimmy Osmond?

In response to your query I can tell you that Jimmy Osmond is now running his own video production company in Salt Lake City, USA. His company specialises in movie titles and video effects. He has unfortunately given up crooning into microphones in public - what a shame!
Ms Jo Burnes
Edinburgh.

Jimmy Osmond:
Who on Earth cares?
M. Crombe
Huddersfield,
West Yorkshire.

He got bigger.
Georgia Lane
Telford, Shropshire.

Well, I can't be sure, but since no one has heard of him for such a long time I wonder if his love life was not all he cracked it up to be. So perhaps he may have jumped into the Mersey, become entangled in his hair and disappeared into the Irish Sea.
Helen Deverill
Salisbury, Wiltshire.

Declining public interest forced little Jimmy Osmond to drastic steps. Radical cosmetic surgery and speech therapy allowed the torment to continue. He is now known as Jason Donovan.
Maureen Begley
Hertfordshire.

FACT!

Thomas Crapper was the inventor of the overhead flushing system toilet.

FACT!

American Indians had no word for America before it was discovered by Christopher Columbus.

CHAPTER

TEN

AND THE REST. . .

What are the chances of aliens making contact with us in the next 100 years?

The chances are pretty low; in fact I'd go so far as to say that they are out of this world!
Miss S. Gilbert
Oxford.

Aliens will no doubt get in touch with us during the next ten decades. Whether they will stay for board and lodging is another matter. What with all the trouble and strife they will most likely get back into their flying saucers and take off to a less contaminated and trouble free planet.
Grace Graham
Birchington, Kent.

There is absolutely no chance since the Aliens Channel at all our airports have been scrapped and replaced by EC or Non-EC Passport Holders Only.
Charles Ottowell
Church Crookham, Hants.

They already have, I've been married to one for the last 23 years.
Mrs Jennifer Bird
Banbury, Oxon.

The chances of making contact are extremely high in view of the fact that the first radio broadcasts from Earth beginning in the 1920's have now reached a radius of seventy light years in distance and they could possibly be picked up by aliens and replied to. Nostradamus's famous prediction that 'In the year 1999 and seven months from the sky shall come an alarmingly powerful king', is widely interpreted as being a prophecy of a visitor from space.
Mr P. Foster
Eastbourne, Sussex.

What are the odds on winning the pools?

The overall chances for winning the pools are very slim. First of all compare how much the overall stakes are returned in winnings in comparison to other forms of legal gambling.

The pools companies return 30 per cent of all stakes as winnings, casinos return 97 per cent, bingo returns are 94 per cent, betting shops around 80 per cent, and slot machines about 70 per cent. It is surprising therefore that the pools is such a popular form of gambling. No doubt people are attracted mainly by the prospect of a huge win for a very small stake.

In real terms this works out at about one win for every 175 coupons sent in. However, this may only be a small win and not the £1M+ we all hope for.
Philip Howarth
Burnley, Lancs.

The chances are pretty slim, but you can take it from me that once you have won the big one you will realise why people do the pools.
Out of interest I did win the big one a few years ago after trying for many years and it was well worth it!
Mr X (for no publicity)
West Midlands.

In my case impossible, I never do them.
Harry Gummer
Rainham, Essex.

The odds on winning the pools is basically an evens bet. A punter either forecasts correctly the correct 8 score draws, or does not forecast them correctly.
Roy Marshall Archer
Dunham on Trent, Notts.

FACT!

The largest inhabited castle in the world is Windsor Castle.

When does a boat become a ship?

According to the *Admiralty Manual of Seamanship Volume 1* a boat becomes a ship when it exceeds 45 feet in length.
S.S. Booth Cdr. RN (Retd)
Chew Stoke, Bristol.

I think it's a question of size. A ship is generally larger than a boat. Similarly a house is larger than a bungalow, but that's another storey!
Janet Burholt
Dorchester, Dorset.

As an ex Merchant Naval Officer it often dismays me when people refer to a ship as a boat. In order to comply with safety regulations all ships must carry a specified number of lifeboats. This is the point at which a boat becomes a ship.
David Rivers
Surbiton, Surrey

The Royal Navy teaches its new entrants that to qualify as a boat, a vessel must have only one continuous deck above one waterline, as opposed to a ship that must have more than one. However, the easiest layman's way to establish if a vessel is a boat or a ship is to remember that a ship may carry a boat but not vice versa.
  Naturally misuse of the term boat where ship is the correct description will succeed in annoying any self-respecting sailor.
C. Gooch
Tamworth, Staffs.

A boat becomes a ship when it's too big to be rowed!
W.H. Davies
Filton, Bristol.

Normally when it's put into a bottle!
Mrs K. Tindale
Parkside, Stafford.

It is claimed that the three most influential inventions of the 20th century are the aeroplane, television, and the atomic bomb. Do you agree?

Gatwick Airport, the on/off switch and cigarettes were introduced to enable us not to be influenced at all by the aeroplane, the television, and the atomic bomb.
Colin Blomeley
Liskeard, Cornwall.

I feel the most influential invention ever is the space rocket. It has opened up so many new possibilities to go forward into places other than our own restrictive planet. The three inventions would be merely of influence in only a speck (or is it spock?) of the universe if it were not for space travel.
A close second is the ability to harness nuclear fusion as this will give us the energy needed to power almost any other earthly invention.
Tom Goodworth
Wrotham, Kent.

With all the satellite, cable, and normal TV channels available today my vote goes to the channel chopper. It's absolutely essential to be able to change channels without walking backwards and forwards to the set.
Our channel chopper slid into the settee once and it was like living in the stone age until we found it. Two other contenders, perhaps, for consideration are the TV Guide and the Off Licence.
Colin Kershaw
Royton, Lancs.

The most influential has to be the personal computer. It has opened up whole new worlds in education, work, and leisure which only a few years ago would have seemed unbelievable.
Jason Ashcroft
Failsworth, Lancs.

The three mentioned purely as inventions cannot be in any way compared to the discovery of the vacuum flask which is truly amazing. Why? Because it manages to keep hot things hot, and cold things cold, and to this day I haven't worked out how it knows the difference.
Robert Parlett
Collingham, Notts.

The three most influential are: the contraceptive pill for giving women control over their destinies; the video for recording programmes you feel you ought to watch, which you conveniently forget to replay; and finally toilet paper made from recycled newsprint - so that the lesser tabloids get the attention they deserve.
Tim Hopkins
Luton, Beds.

The atomic bomb should have been loaded onto the aeroplane and dropped on the television.
Theresa Murphy
Giant's Head Farm, Dorset.

The invention that will end up as being probably the most influential is that of the chainsaw, because without it the millions of square miles of forest around the world would still be intact.
P. Brennan
Great Easton, Leics.

It's got to be the plastic cover that fits over a child's pushchair. Now, for the first time in history children can explore the world and gain the knowledge they need about it, regardless of how inclement the weather may be.
Joy Hindley
New Moston, Manchester.

FACT!

The brain consists of more water than human blood.

FACT!

The word 'and' appears in the Bible 46,227 times.

What should I tell my children when they ask me who made God?

I tell my children that no one made God, as, like a circle, He has no beginning and no end.
Brady Vanam
Glasgow.

The answer is obvious (being 'non-made' is part of what 'God' means). The problem is getting that across to children. Actually the real problem is getting it across to adults - in a technological age there is a spiritual hole in our outlook. Try (1) talking about love and happiness in the home: that's not 'made' and it's the best thing we've got - it's like God. (2) Try worshipping together: you don't stop asking the wrong questions until you experience what you are talking about!
Father Terence McCann
Manchester.

I told my children that no person on earth knew the real answer and that if they worked hard and tried to understand the many things they were taught, then one day they could be the people to give the real answer to such a difficult question.
It may not have answered the direct question itself from the children, but it certainly inspired them to learn more about the world for themselves.
Katriona McConnachy
Carlisle, Cumbria.

It is so strange but whenever my children ask me a question like that it nearly always coincides with something boiling over in the kitchen that I must urgently go and attend to.
Christine Kelly
Aylesbury, Bucks.

Why do doctors and nurses wear green in an operating theatre?

Psychologists have discovered that the colours in our working environment have a definite impact on our performance. The colour green (along with blue) is the most popular and effective for encouraging efficient work and a patient's harmonious attitude. Whether or not the selection of green for operating theatre` dress was deliberate, research has shown it to be the right choice.

Tim Hopkins
Luton, Beds.

Doctors and nurses wear green in the operating theatre to match the colour of the patients.

Mandeep Ahluwalia
Sidcup, Kent.

Green is the predominant colour of clothing in an operating theatre because it is the complementary colour of red (blood). Complementary colours when mixed together produce a murky brown-green whilst when placed side to side produce violent contrasts. The effect of this is to concentrate the eye on the operating site which stands out brilliantly from the surrounding green which yet remains murky and dull even if blood spills on it.

Dr K. Ghattas
Harley Street, London.

The majority of theatre sterile gowns and drapes are green; some are blue. This is because, as 'discovered' by plants, green and blue absorb the most light. These colours are used to reduce the reflective glare from the strong overhead operating lights. This ensures that the open wound remains the centre of attraction.

Dr Mark B. Smith
Hardwick, Cambridge.

Is it true that the organ music in the 1967 Procol Harum hit *Whiter Shade of Pale* was composed by Bach, or based on one of his compositions? If so, which one?

It is based on the second movement of J.S. Bach's 3rd Orchestral Suite in D, a set of dance tunes arranged for a small orchestra. The movement is sometimes known as *Air on a G String*.
Graham Hewitt
Rowley Regis, West Midlands.

According to the *A-Z of the 1960's* by Ann and Ian Morrison, the music was based on Bach's *Air on a G String*. The song is based on a poem by Keith Reid who was responsible for forming the group, although he did not play in it. The meaning of the lyrics have never been fully explained, but probably refers to what the subconscious undergoes when under the influence of drugs.
Mrs R. Bircher
Quedgeley, Gloucester.

CASPARED?

If the chairman of a company is left handed is his number one assistant his left hand man?

FACT!

It is possible to tell the approximate age of a fish by counting the rings found on its scales.

What constitutes a massacre? As only eleven people were killed in the Peterloo Massacre it must be more than a matter of numbers.

The Peterloo Massacre followed an 80,000 strong meeting held at St. Peter's Field, Manchester, to demand parliamentary reform. Eleven people were killed and about 400 injured when the cavalry moved in to disperse the crowd. This incident led to great indignation throughout Britain, epitomised in the way that the riot was linked to the Battle of Waterloo in the satirical title the Peterloo Massacre. It was not a true massacre, merely an example of 19th century propaganda.
Elspeth Jones
Thorpe Bay, Essex.

The dictionary definition of a massacre is 'indiscriminate killing of unresisting people; indiscriminate slaughter with barbarity'. Therefore the number killed is not important, but the fact that they are unresisting is.
Dinah Porter
Rochester, Kent.

Certainly not, eleven persons are just right. It happens to Brighton F.C. every away fixture they play.
Les Bailey
Seaford, East Sussex.

FACT!

The first horse racing photofinish was at Epsom in 1947.

Would it be possible to split time into metric units and would there be any advantage in doing so?

In theory it is quite possible to split time into metric units, probably a hundred second minute, a hundred second hour, and a 10 hour day. This would at a stroke eliminate all the problems of AM/PM and the 12/24 hour clock confusions.

The *eventual* advantages would be tremendous, vastly simplifying all calculations where time is a function, and probably enabling even adults to preprogramme video recorders.

However, the practical difficulties make such a change unlikely.

Initially the length of the 'official second' would have to be redesignated to .864 of our existing second. Then every physical constant involving time would need to be updated accordingly from speed limits to pulse rates. Also of course virtually every piece of equipment in the world related to time would have to be scrapped and replaced, together with printed details ranging from technical books to the numbers on car speedometers. This would also include your watch, clock, and egg-timer.

And anyway, within ten new minutes British Rail would announce a 105 minute hour.

Chris Shipp
Kingsbridge, Devon.

FACT!

Tokyo has more restaurants than any other city in the world, with an unbelievable figure of over a quarter of a million.

Time is already split into metric units for the purpose of calculating children's growth rates in paediatric height and weight standard charts.

The system of decimal age is used in these charts, with the year being divided into ten, not twelve segments. Each date of the calendar is marked in terms of thousandths of a year, thus 6 July 1991 is 91.510. The child's birthdate is similarly recorded e.g. child born on 7 January 1991 is 91.016. Age at examination (say 6 July 1991) is obtained by simple extraction, i.e.:

91.510 minus 91.016 equals 0.494

with the last figure being rounded off.

This system greatly facilitates the computing of growth rates, since the proportion of the year between two examinations is easily calculated.

James McTavish
Addenbrookes Hospital
Cambridge.

FACT!

Snakes hear sound by picking up sound waves from their tongues.

FACT!

It is easier to die from lack of sleep than from lack of food.

FACT!

The Isle of Man was under the sovereignty of Norway until 1266.

FACT!

The average age for a woman to undergo childbirth in the United Kingdom is 27 years.

FACT!

All members of parliament are exempt from jury service.

If I said 'I always tell lies', would I be telling the truth?

The person saying 'I always tell lies' either absolutely has to tell lies, or doesn't. For the absolute liar, 'I always tell lies' would itself have to be a lie, the truth of the matter therefore being 'I never tell lies'. It is therefore simply impossible for a person who really does always lie to say so, there is no true or false in the matter, the statement coming from an absolute liar's lips is as logically impossible as 'black is white'. On the other hand, if the speaker doesn't have to lie, but is simply a habitual liar, the statement is meaningful and even truthful. Here, the statement is intended as truth, as it doesn't really refer to itself through the 'always'. The problem, then, only arises because of a blurring of how we ordinarily use 'always' (e.g. 'It always rains on Sundays') and what 'always' strictly entails.

Mr G. E. Davies
Bromley, Kent.

Yes - if I'm a politician!
P. McFarlane
Totland, Isle of Wight.

If you were always telling lies you would not be telling the truth because` you would be lying, wouldn't you.
Christopher Brown
Aylesbury, Bucks.

The answer to the question depends on the circumstances. If you are telling the truth when you say 'I always tell lies' then it is true that you are lying. But how can you be lying if you are telling the truth? However, if you are lying when you say 'I always tell lies' then you are telling the truth. But if you are a liar, how can you be telling the truth? If you are lying when you say 'I always tell lies' this means you do not always tell lies. So sometimes you tell the truth.
Miss Kelly Hignett
Oswestry, Shropshire.

How much man-made debris is whistling around in space?

Very little I'm afraid. You see, space is either a vacuum or a near-vacuum and a body needs a good lungful of air in order to whistle.

Sounds, as you know, are a vibration of the air, so in a vacuum there would be no noise. This is one of the main reasons why Larry Adler has never performed in space.
Mr E. J. Wilson
Durham.

Since Sputnik I was launched in 1957, man has managed to leave 20,844 trackable objects still in earth orbit or deeper space. Of these 14,163 are large pieces of debris, mainly rocket stages. The remaining 6,681 objects are mainly satellites and spacecraft. There are also reckoned to be a few million untrackable pieces of debris.
Derek Mellor
Cheltenham,
Gloucestershire.

Just to give you an idea of how much space debris there actually is in space, figures from early 1992 show that the USSR has a total of 10,740 objects, the USA 3,374 and the European Space Agency 438.

The worrying thing is that even so-called developing nations such as Pakistan, India, Indonesia and many others also are responsible for numerous bits of unwanted and potentially dangerous space rubbish.
B. Williams
Stockport, Cheshire.

Because of the vast amounts of debris circling the Earth, it has been said that astronomer Sir Bernard Lovell believes the Earth will soon look like the planet Saturn with its familiar rings around it, especially if the Russian cosmonauts continue to push bags of rubbish into space as they routinely do now!
George Dunk
Cleveland.

Could a symphony orchestra give a good performance without a conductor?

Yes, it could, and it has done so. I have a recording, dating from the 1950's, of Dvorak's Fifth Symphony played by the 'Orchestra of the Air'. This was the orchestra conducted by Arturo Toscanini which, as a tribute to his memory, made this recording on the first anniversary of his death. I doubt if many people, except perhaps a few conductors or leaders, could tell there was no conductor.
Peter Summersgill,
Oxshott, Surrey.

In the town of Merthyr Tydfil, 119 buses an hour leave the local terminus without even one conductor. This being the case, I am convinced an intelligent symphony orchestra could manage similarly.
Mr C. Foy
Ponteland, Northumberland.

My friend and I are agreed it would not be a good performance. The reason is that although all the musicians would undoubtedly be first class in the execution of their performance on their particular instrument, the performance is not only one of skill in getting the right notes but of feel and interpretation of the music. You have only to listen to performances by different conductors to see the variations in time and interpretation.
Without a conductor everyone would play at what they felt to be the right speed. They would all have different ideas about pauses and about rallentandos and crescendos. With 120 players in an orchestra there would probably be chaos!
Mrs D. M. Spencer
Croydon, Surrey.

How on earth do you weigh a ship?

The register ton used to describe the size of a ship is not a measure of weight but of volume, a register ton being equal to 100 cubic feet. The term is derived from the number of tuns or casks which could be stowed on a medieval ship.

The figure usually cited is the gross register ton. Deducting all the spaces used for manning and operating the ship gives the net register ton. The shipowner pays his dues for the use of docks, pilots, tugs, and lighthouses at so much per net ton.

A ship's deadweight tonnage is measured by the weight of the cargo she can carry. Thus a passenger liner has a large gross tonnage but a small deadweight while a bulk carrier or tanker has a comparatively small gross tonnage but a massive deadweight.

Warships, which carry neither passengers nor cargo, are described by their displacement tonnage - the amount of water they occupy using Archimedes' Principle.

Mr C. H. Milsom
Upton, Merseyside.

The weight of a ship is one of several ways of describing the size of the vessel. It is measured, not by physically weighing the ship, but by calculating the volume of the hull that will be under the water when the ship is afloat. By Archimedes' Principle, a floating body displaces its own weight in water and so this underwater volume, when multiplied by the density of seawater, will yield the displacement tonnage: the weight of the ship.

Lt. Cdr. Geoffrey Carr, CEng, FIMarE, RN
Melksham, Wiltshire.

Surely everyone knows, you never actually weigh the ship, just the anchor!

Mr J. A. Tilling
Ardington, Oxon.

I am reliably informed that each individual part of the *Titanic* was weighed (nuts, bolts, nails, hinges, etc, by the pound) before assembly. The figures were then entered into a log, which ran to 1,461 pages. The weights of each item were then totalled to reach the final tonnage. This task was performed by five people, working ten hours a day for three weeks.
Anne Britten
St. Albans, Herts.

Simple - you sail the ship into the middle of a large school of fish and then weigh it on their scales.
Basil Sargent
Reigate, Surrey.

You stand on the bathroom scales with it and then subtract your own weight from the total.
Holly Trundell
Edinburgh.

FACT!

Millionaire filmstar Sylvester Stallone was paid the sum of 25 T-shirts for his first lead role in a film.

FACT!

Ants are capable of lifting 50 times their own weight.

FACT!

There are only about 4000 bottle banks in the United Kingdom.

FACT!

In 1989 a 70-year-old American woman lost several feet of her small intestine after flushing the vacuum toilet on a cruise liner whilst still seated.

CASPARED?

Why does bread and butter always fall butterside down?

CASPARED?

Why do women who claim to dislike men always seem to look and dress like them?

What would be the outcome if a government won a general election, but the prime minister lost his seat?

Firstly, according to the Constitution of the United Kingdom, in a general election, voters in individual constituencies all over the UK vote for their MP, and ultimately decide the political make-up of the House of Commons, when all the MPs are totalled. The voters do not elect a prime minister, as we are a parliamentary democracy, rather than a presidential democracy. The Queen summons the leader of the largest party in the House of Commons, and invites him/her to become prime minister. If the leader of that party loses his/her House of Commons seat, then that is essentially a party matter, as the party won the election. The Queen would summon another senior member of the party, say Foreign Secretary or Chancellor to act as 'caretaker prime minister', while the governing party began the process to elect a new leader, who, once elected, would become prime minister automatically.
Mark Russell
Richhill, County Armagh.

If such a thing happened it would obviously be a MAJOR upset!
Maurice Brown
Gossops Green, Sussex.

The ex-prime minister would probably land himself a cushy job as governor of some far flung colony until he could be re-elected at the next safe by-election.
Andy Haddleton
London NW10.

If the Prime Minister lost his seat then he, or she, would be left standing, of course.
J. Lawrence
Edinburgh.

How many wars are being fought around the world at this moment?

According to the news there are no wars going on at the moment - they are all conflicts.
David Scatcherd
Mansfield, Notts.

Just count the country stamps on Kate Adie's passport!
Mrs F. Ranger
Wenvoe, Cardiff.

My best estimate is two. Too many.
Steve Hall
Mildenhall, Suffolk.

The exact number is impossible to determine since apart from the major wars taking place, there are those who would no doubt claim that many sectarian conflicts throughout our planet are also 'war'.
It is obviously a fact that wars have increased alarmingly during our century. Statistics show that during the 18th century war deaths totalled about 4.4 million. This rose to 8.3 million in the 19th century and during this century so far, war has claimed over 100 million lives.
Mrs G. McGuinness
Robertsbridge, East Sussex.

FACT!

The largest living thing on Earth is not the blue whale as is commonly believed but instead the giant sequoia tree, commonly found in North America.

FACT!

Bob Dylan took his stage name from the poet Dylan Thomas.

How fast is Warp Factor 9 in *Star Trek*?

Zefram Cochrane was the pioneer of the warp drive system. The units measuring sub space stress (the warp field) are called cochranes. Cochranes are also used to measure field distortion created by other spatial manipulation devices, including tractor beams, deflectors and synthetic gravity fields. Any fields below warp one are measured in millicochranes. The approximate values of warp factors are:
(C = Cochrane / Speed of Light)
Warp factor 1 = 1 C
Warp factor 2 = 10 C
Warp factor 3 = 39 C
Warp factor 4 = 102 C
Warp factor 5 = 214 C
Warp factor 6 = 392 C
Warp factor 7 = 656 C
Warp factor 8 = 1024 C
Warp factor 9 = 1516 C
Warp factor 10 can never be reached as this is infinite speed.
Ian Williams
Halesowen, West Midlands.

In the legend that is *Star Trek*, little mention in the series is made as to how fast the various warp factors actually are. All we know is that they represent faster than light speeds, and the higher the factor the more Scotty complained. The U.S.S. Enterprise NCC 1701 in the original series, normal top speed was warp 9 although in the episode 'Is There in Truth No Beauty?' it reached warp 14.1. Off screen, the definition of warp speed became the cube of the factor being equal to the number of times faster than light the ship was travelling. So for warp 1, Enterprise was travelling just faster than light. Warp 2 equalled 8 times the speed of light and so forth. Warp 9 was 729 times the speed light.
For *Star Trek: the Next Generation*, the warp scale was recalibrated for Enterprise NCC 1701 D with warp 10 being infinite speed, and warp factors appearing

on a curved graph increasing sharply after warp 9.6. Warp 1 is still close to the speed of light, but warp 9 is equal to 1516 times the speed of light. (The actual speed is affected by the spatial distortion of mass of interstellar objects.) Enterprise D equalled Kirk's ship's warp 14.1 on the old scale at warp 9.7 on the new in *Encounter at Farpoint*, and reached warp 9.9999999999.6 in 'Where No One Has Gone Before' (with assistance).
Ric Knott
Wraysbury, Middlesex.

Warp factor 9 was just fast enough to hurl all the members of the cast around the bridge, accompanied by screams of terror, loud sirens and Scotty yelling 'She canna take any more Captain!' Perhaps they should have fitted seat belts.
Carol Youlton
Ashton under Lyne, Lancs.

By the look of Spock's ears I would assume warp factor 9 must be very fast indeed!
Mark Crean
Covent Garden, London.

FACT!

Britain's greatest naval hero Admiral Lord Horatio Nelson was reputed to have suffered continually through his career from sea sickness.

FACT!

Over 20 million bees were used as 'extras' in the shooting of the film 'The Swarm in 1978

FACT!

In the past two hundred years there has never been a confirmed account of an avalanche being set off by somebody shouting.

FACT!

Although we normally think of rainbows as being curved and multicoloured, it is possible to see rainbows that are all purple, all red, all white, and even straight and vertical ones.

Are there any areas in which Britain still leads the world?

Aside from the negative things such as mad cow disease, football violence, repossessions, bankruptcies, etc. there are still a few things for which we can be proud.

Our music industry is second to none, with British bands topping the charts of nearly every western nation on a regular basis. In the world of design we are actually exporting our talent to other countries desperate for our knowledge and flair. If this isn't enough we are winning the race for 'cold' fusion, which should bring cheaper energy to a needy world.

We may not be as great as we once were but we still have the ability to be leaders in literally hundreds of areas right across the spectrum from genetic engineering and chemicals through to advertising and financial services.

Johnathan Wood
Burnley, Lancs.

The only one area of endeavour in which Britain leads the world, is its adherence to the foolish belief that Britain still leads the world in everything.
A. Hughes
Warrington.

Yes, many. At the top go Freedom of the Individual and Foreign Affairs.
N. Richards
Redditch, Worcestershire.

Yes. There is research going on in all areas of life, sciences and electronics at universities and scientific establishments throughout Britain. However, nothing ever developed is implemented as funding is dropped. This tends to lead us to import from abroad an invention or system which was tested in Britain (but never marketed) at a higher cost to us than if it had been installed after its final testing.
Mr A. F. Heaton
Preston.

What name will be given to the decade 2000 to 2010?

The decade will be known as the Noughties. They might even come to be remembered as the naughty noughties.
Lynn Davies
Rochester, Kent.

After the Seventies, Eighties and Nineties, why not carry on with this trend and call the decade from the year 2000 to 2010 the Tens?
Jonathan Derry,
Chester.

I'm sure I'm not the only one to point out that the decade DOES start at 2000 and lasts until 2009 i.e. ten years. It is the new century (or in this case, millennium) which does not start until 2001.
  As to giving this period a name, the period of 1900-1909 was called the 1900's, so I suppose the 2000's seems to be most likely.
Sean Hayne
Huddersfield.

Should the divorce rate continue to rise, then the 'singles' would seem appropriate.
Mrs L.M. Callander
Wallasey, Merseyside.

Nearly 6 million of us will be over 75 by that time, so obviously, the Grecian 2000's.
Jean Hay
London SW6.

FACT!

The only animal able to turn its stomach inside out is the starfish.

FACT!

In 1896 a war between the United Kingdom and Zanzibar lasted 38 minutes.

Where did all the earth dug from London's Underground go to?

I can tell you where some of it went. When Chelsea Football Club was formed in 1905 and Stamford Bridge became their home, the biggest job, and the most urgent, was to build a huge mound for the purposes of terracing.

It was composed mostly of clay excavated during the construction of the Piccadilly Line which runs closest to Chelsea's ground at Earl's Court.

That wide-open terracing used to hold 40,000 spectators. It has since been replaced by the West stand.
Albert Sewell
Greenford, Middlesex.

The earth from the building of the Underground system was used to make the Thames Embankment. The latter was necessary to a) make the Thames narrower and deeper (to allow larger ships to pass through it) and b) to cover the new sewage system which was constructed from the various minor tributaries of the Thames and the already-existing open sewers which went down to its shores.
Mrs Alison Young
Hampton.

The first earth dug out for tunnels filled worn out clay pits and brickfields in and around London.
F.A. Tomkins
Wivenhoe, Essex.

It came to an area called Brookfield Farm in Lower Edmonton, which, back in the 1920's was a low lying valley.

Now in the 1990's, our houses are subsiding as the clay dries out, and gardeners are still trying to come to terms with all the underground subsoil.

I know from experience; my house is built on the stuff!
Mrs J.P. McClean
Lower Edmonton, London.

Local legend has it that the soil went to form a clay hill in Basildon, Essex. This explains why there is a massive mound in the middle of otherwise flat land.
Rosemary Mullender
Billericay, Essex.

It was stock-piled in Hackney, then, being almost pure clay, it was used in the manufacture of bricks. So what was once below ground is now above ground!
Ronald Sweet
Oswestry, Shropshire.

GEEEE..... You mean her majesty actually walked on this here mud ?!

Who selects the music played in supermarkets?

Every supermarket has a dungeon housing a staff of deaf and dumb troglodytes especially trained to make random selections of cassettes.
George Crosby
Weston-super-Mare.

If my local Tesco is anything to go by, it is probably someone from Sainsbury's. The choice of Cliff Richard's *Mistletoe and Wine* last Christmas sent customers away from the food section in droves.
Jenny Smith
Bristol, Avon.

Whoever it is, they must be 'off their trolley'. Most of the music is certainly past its 'sell-by date!'
John Sherriff
Coventry, West Midlands.

Reg Holdsworth from the sound of it.
Mr S. J. Collins
Ashbrooke, Sunderland,

I dislike 'muzak' so much I wrote complaining to the manager of my local Asda. I was informed that the reason for this mind blowing rubbish is that wherever music is played in public the Performing Rights Society receive payment on behalf of the composers. When played on a large scale such as in supermarkets nationwide, the fee comes to a tidy sum. To get round this there are companies that employ orchestras and unknown singers and composers who get a lump sum for singing, playing and writing these 'mean' tunes played in the stores. This obviously makes a considerable saving on Performing Rights. In effect nobody actually chooses the tapes they are just sent out on a regular basis to the various supermarkets.
Yvonne A. Kenny
Pevensey Bay, East Sussex.